Zacharias Tanee Fomum

Enjoying the Choice of Your Marriage Partner

Éditions du Livre Chrétien
4, rue du Révérend Père Cloarec
92400 Courbevoie France
editionlivrechretien@gmail.com

First Edition. 1984, 3000 Copies

Printed by:

Éditions du livre chrétien

4, rue du Révérend Père Cloarec

92400 Courbevoie - FRANCE

Tél: (33) 9 52 29 27 72

Email: editionlivrechretien@gmail.com

Covert by:

Jacques Maré

I dedicate this book to

my darling wife **Prisca**

and our beloved children

Ruth Angum

Paul Tanee

Stephen Fokam

Elizabeth Afor

John Sentamu

in grateful acknowledgement of their constant

love and encouragement.

Table of Contents

Foreword

Many marriages end in divorce, and even those that do not end in physical separation are largely broken. Many people are just managing to keep it up because the laws of society demand it, or because of the children. Many people discover in the marriage relationship that they made a tragic mistake. They married the wrong person. They made an irreversible mistake in their choice.

The crucial prerequisite for a happy marriage is that both parties be in the centre of God's will for them; that they be rightly related to God, understand what God wants marriage to be, and be committed to that purpose. It also demands that the partners know themselves, know what they want in the partner, look for the right person and make the right choice. After the choice has been made, the relationship needs also to be rightly handled for it to truly succeed.

We believe that God meant marriage to be a wonderful experience – a foretaste of heaven on earth. We believe that He has the right partner for you and that if you co-operate with Him, you will find that partner and be truly blessed. The question is, "Who is that partner? How can I find him/her? How can we carry out our relationship so that it remains a blessing?" This book will tell you.

ENJOYING THE CHOICE OF YOUR MARRIAGE PART-NER is the second book in the series, "God, Sex and You." Book One in this series is entitled: ENJOYING THE SEXUAL LIFE and Book Three is entitled: ENJOYING THE MARRIED LIFE. Be sure to read all the three books in order to obtain the complete picture.

If this book has blessed, encouraged or angered and frustrated you, be sure to write and let me know. Please write at once. Do not wait for tomorrow.

We send this book out with prayer that it should become your book. Read it. Secure a copy for a friend.

God bless you!

Yaoundé,
1984

Zacharias Tanee Fomum
PO. Box 6090
Yaoundé – Cameroun

I made a terrible mistake !

We had been married for three months when I started comparing her with other girls whose tender care I had discouraged. She was not as hard-working as Monique or Chantal. She neither had the wit nor the sense of humour of Marie-Claire or Suzanne. She was far from being as sensuous as Sylvie or Dorotha. She lacked this and she lacked that. I was bored with her. I had made the wrong choice. It was the drama of my life. I needed to divorce her before it was too late. I kept thinking…

* * *

It was 2am. I had had a long session in the Clinic for Spiritual Diseases with a couple. It was a hard time. The session had begun at 10pm. It was four hours of agony. She said to me, "Dr. Fomum, I am unfortunate." Then she burst into loud sobs and cried for a long time. "I am unfortunate. I wish I had listened. This man is utterly useless. I do not see one good thing in him. I wish I had listened." She continued weeping. She was pregnant. The marriage certificate had just recently been signed. She was deeply frustrated. I looked at the man. He was handsome. He had a good job. I told her, "Surely there are many good things in him. He is handsome." And I tried to point out as many good things about him as were immediately obvious. But she cried on and on and said, "There is nothing beyond the surface. I am ruined. I wish I had a second chance… I have made the mistake of my life and now I must bear it. How will I stand it for all these years? I wish I could die and end it all…"

* * *

He was well placed. She was educated and sophisticated. They had been married for 16 years. They had children. They had possessions. They had position. Then she came for counselling and this is what she said, "I knew from the beginning that it would not work. I always felt that I should say, "No", but I did not. Then we got married, and it has been sixteen years in hell."

* * *

"At the beginning he begged me. He did everything I wanted. I turned him round my small finger. Each time we quarrelled, he was the one who always did everything to re-establish the relationship. He bought me gifts. He gave me everything I wanted. I gave him nothing. I had deep reservations in my heart. I knew I could never be fulfilled with him. He lacked something I could not describe. He just could never pull me out and satisfy me. However, I was very flattered by the fact that he gave me everything. So I decided I would marry him for the joy of having a worshipper around me to supply my needs. Then we got married, and he turned into a tiger! I had the misery of being forced to run after him to be given even an embrace. I wish I had known better."

* * *

"It was all arranged by my relatives. He was many years older than me. He was experienced in every way. I was only 17. When I saw him I did not like his appearance, although he was quite handsome. We were married. All through it I never loved him. He loved me and was interested in other women too. I only gave myself to him when I wanted something out of him. There was another man. I loved and respected him. He would have been my ideal husband. He also loved and respected me. It was all pure, but we were from different tribes…"

* * *

"We had grown up in the same village and were friends. We were the same age. I told her I would marry her. She accepted. That was twelve years ago. I went to the secondary school. She did two years of post primary education and became a village primary school teacher. I went to the high school. We continued to correspond with each other. I entered the University to study medicine. Now I have finished my housemanship. She is still the village teacher. She does not understand me. I do not understand her. I still love her, but it is not the liking that has desire. She is to me like my sister and friend. She is anxiously waiting for me. Years ago I knew that I could not marry her, but I did not have the courage to tell her. I was afraid that it would hurt her. But in my heart the relationship was finished." Then he said to me, "Look at her letter. Read this part of it." I drew near and read it: "Oh! Darling, I've waited and waited for these years and now my dream is about to be fulfilled. When are you coming? Everything in me is burning. Come quickly. Every minute that now separates me from you is unbearable. We shall be married immediately. All my savings are yours to use as you like and, of course, I am all yours. The money is enough to pay for the bride price and all the expenses of the wedding. There will be enough left for us to live on until you start working. So let nothing worry you. Come at once. Send me a telegram as to your flight. My parents and I will be at the airport to welcome you. Come, my dear. Come, my king. I am waiting and I am longing..." Then he said, "Dr. Fomum, that is my problem. I wish I had told her the truth years ago. What shall I do?"

* * *

MARRIAGE AS GOD MEANT IT TO BE

CHAPTER I

God, the author of marriage

Marriage originated in the mind of God. The Bible says, *"Then the Lord God said, 'It is not good that the man should be alone; I will make him a helper fit for him.' So out of the ground the Lord God formed every beast of the field and every bird of the air, and brought them to the man to see what he would call them; and whatever the man called every living creature, that was its name. The man gave names to all cattle, and to the birds of the air, and to every beast of the field; but for man there was not found a helper fit for him. So the Lord God caused a deep sleep to fall upon the man, and while he slept took one of his ribs and closed up its place with flesh, and the rib which the Lord God had taken from the man he made into a woman and brought her to the man. Then the man said, 'This at last is bone of my bones and flesh of my flesh; she shall be called Woman, because she was taken out of Man.' Therefore a man leaves his father and his mother and cleaves to his wife, and they become one flesh"* (Genesis 2:18-24).

So we see that marriage began in the mind of God. He brought the first marriage into being. It was not an action forced on Him. He was not compelled to make a wife for Adam. He did it in His own will. That is how it was at the very beginning. It was a wonderful marriage. He was the Author.

Today, God is still at work in His universe. He longs to say to Himself about you, "It is not good that so and so should be alone; I will make him a helper fit for him."

When God causes a man to be what He meant him to be and transforms a woman into what He meant her to be, and then brings together a particularly transformed man and a specially transformed woman whom He created to be that man's helper fit, then marriage is contracted with Him as its Author.

CHAPTER 2

The creation of man

Man is not a purposeless being that came out of nowhere. God created man. The Bible says, *"These are the generations of the heavens and the earth when they were created. In the day that the Lord God made the earth and the heavens, when no plant of the field was yet in the earth and no herb of the field had yet sprung up - for the Lord God had not caused it to rain upon the earth, and there was no man to till the ground; but a mist went up from the earth and watered the whole face of the ground – then the Lord God formed man of dust from the ground, and breathed into his nostrils the breath of life; and man became a living being. And the Lord God planted a garden in Eden, in the east; and there he put the man whom he had formed. And out of the ground the Lord God made to grow every tree that is pleasant to the sight and good for food, the tree of life also in the midst of the garden, and the tree of the knowledge of good and evil"* (Genesis 2:4-9).

So we see that God created man. There was a difference between the creation of man and that of the plants of the field or the birds of the air, and so forth. For these there was no special relationship between them and Him. He just created them. He put nothing of Himself into them except His art.

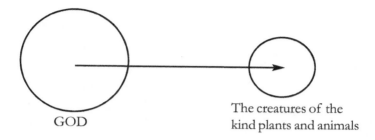

GOD

The creatures of the
kind plants and animals

*Fig. 1: There was no special relationship between God and the other things
He created. He put nothing of himself into them except His art. Such creatures just possess biological life or, in some cases, all they have is chemical
life. The relationship between the Creator (God) and these creatures is like
the relationship between a carpenter and the chair that he has made. The
chair is the product of his art but it possesses no special relationship to him.
It cannot on its own desire him or have a relationship with him.*

However, in the creation of man, God did something special.
After He had formed man, He breathed into man's nostrils the
breath of life and man became a living being. Man, therefore,
possessed biological life along with the rest of creation and, in
addition, he possessed spiritual life as a result of the breath of
God.

The breath of God (it can also be considered as the Spirit of
God) dwelt in man, controlling man and enabling man to relate
properly to God. There was, therefore, a vital fellowship between
God and man. God could communicate His thoughts and purposes to man, and man could respond fully to God. Man possessed an inward capacity to desire God and to seek Him.

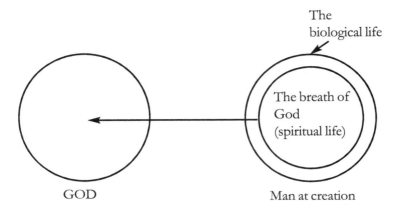

Fig. 2: Man possessed biological life and spiritual life, and God was spe-cially related to man because His breath dwelt in man.

CHAPTER 3

Why did God create man ?

We have seen that God created man in a very special way. We have also seen that there was a vital relationship between God and man. Why did God do this? Was He just interested in producing someone who was different from the rest of His creation? The answer is obviously, "No." He was not out for fun or for variety. He had a special purpose for man. That purpose is put forth as follows: *"Be fruitful and multiply, and fill the earth and subdue it; and have dominion over the fish of the sea and over the birds of the air and over every living thing that moves upon the earth"* (Genesis 1.28). *"The Lord God took the man and put him in the garden of Eden to till it and keep it"* (Genesis 2.15). We can summarize it by saying that God created man so that man should:

-   Be fruitful and multiply and fill the earth.
-   Subdue the earth.
-   Have dominion over: the fish of the sea, the birds of the air, every living thing that moves upon the earth.
-   Till the garden and keep it.

So God's purpose in creating man was to have a co-worker who would co-operate with Him to carry out His (God's) work for His (God's) glory in His (God's) timing. So man was created not to satisfy the needs of man, but to satisfy the "needs" of God.

We conclude, therefore, that whenever man leaves God aside,

leaves the "needs", plans and purposes of God aside, all that he does will fall out of harmony, not only with God, but with himself.

So God created man to do a particular work of God for God.

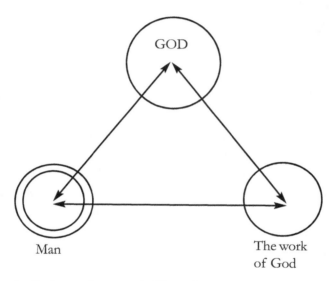

Fig. 3 : God created man to do His work.

So, there was God and God's work and then there was man who was to do God's work. Man was to live in vital fellowship with God and draw from Him the power to do His work.

God's work was to be done in God's way.
God's work was to be done in God's timing.
God's work was to be done in vital fellowship with Him.
God's work was to be done in God's power.

God's work was to be done for the glory of God and for His glory only.

Man was not to do God's work for his own glory or to do God's work partly for God's glory and partly for his own glory.

The extent to which God's work was done was dependent upon the degree of intimacy between man and God, and the extent to which God's purpose was understood and complied with.

CHAPTER 4

The need for a wife

After God had made man and given him His work to do for Him, God soon found that man could not accomplish God's work as he was. There was a need for a helper. Man was alone and needed a companion who would help him to do God's work.

We insist that the need for a wife was a need for a partner who could help man to accomplish God's work. It was of a lonely, labouring man that God said, *"It is not good that man should be alone; I will make him a helper fit for him"* (Genesis 2.18). The helper had to be a compatible helper, not just any helper. She had to be fit to help do God's work.

In God's original purpose, marriage was the acquisition of a helper fit to help man to accomplish God's work. Without God's work, there would therefore be no reason for a helper.

God intends a wife to be a helper fit to help a man to do His work.

A. THE SEARCH FOR A HELPER FIT

God is not a dreamer or a theorizer. He saw that man needed a helper fit to help him to accomplish His purposes. He did not leave things there. He went out to put what He saw into action. He began to look for the helper fit for man. He could have added something to His relationship with man so that man would be able to accomplish His work without the need for a helper.

However, He did not do so. He decided to look for someone else, apart from Himself, yet one in vital relationship with Himself to accomplish this need.

So serious was the task of finding a compatible partner that even God did not find it easy. There was a seeking process and an elimination process. The Bible says, *"Then the Lord God said, 'It is not good that man should be alone; I will make him a helper fit for him.' So out of the ground the Lord God formed every beast of the field and every bird of the air, and brought them to the man to see what he would call them; and whatever the man called every living creature, that was its name. The man gave names to all cattle, and to the birds of the air, and to every beast of the field; but for the man there was not found a helper fit for him. So the Lord God caused a deep sleep to fall upon the man, and while he slept took one of his ribs and closed up its place with flesh; and the rib which the Lord God had taken from the man he made into a woman and brought her to the man. Then the man said, 'This at last is bone of my bones and flesh of my flesh; she shall be called Woman, because she was taken out of Man'"* (Genesis 2:18-23).

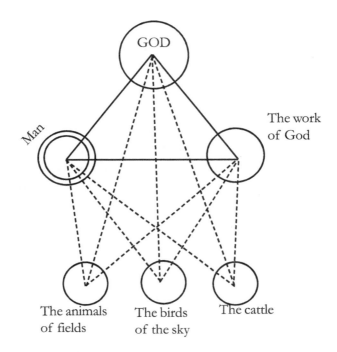

Fig. 4 : Neither the beast of the field, nor the birds of the air, nor the cattle of the field could become the helper fit for man because :
  - They were related to God only in a passive way as creatures and Creator.
  - They were not able to enter into the fullest fellowship with man.
  - They were only passively related to the work of God. They did not have it as an active goal to do the work of God for God's glory.

Anyone who has not received God's new nature given to man through "rebirth by the Spirit of God" will not relate to God as he should. He will also not relate to man as he should, nor will he commit himself without reservation to doing God's work for God's glory. He is in some ways like a beast of the field, a bird of the air or cattle of the field.

We have said that when God decided to make a helper fit for

man, He did not find the process of choosing easy. There was a seeking process and an elimination process. The Lord did not impose His own choice on man; rather, He brought various possibilities to man and allowed man to be the final decider in the whole matter. For example, out of the ground, the Lord God formed every beast of the field and brought them to Adam to see how he could call them. He coolly gave them names and that was all. There was some relationship between man and these beasts of the field, but it was not enough. The next thing that the Lord did was to form every bird of the air and bring them to man. The reaction was the same. He gave them names but was not fully involved with them. Thirdly, the Lord formed all the cattle of the field and brought them to Adam, and he treated them just as he had treated the other creatures. So, at this point, God had brought the following groups of creatures to man to see if he would find his helper fit amongst them:

- Every beast of the field,
- Every bird of the air.,
- Every cattle of the field.

As we have seen, God did not dictate to man whom he was to choose. He presented the possibilities to man and left it to man to decide. God, thereby, gave man total freedom as to whom he could have as his helper.

It is interesting to know that although every beast, bird and cattle had been presented to man, and although man named each one of them and thus indicated that he could have some relationship with them and also find some use for them in the work to which God had called him, the Bible nevertheless says, "But for man there was not found a helper fit for him." The Bible does not say, "But for man there was not found a helper for him." The beast of the field, the birds of the air and the cattle of the field were helpers, but they were not helpers fit for man.

There had to be a helper, and the helper that man was looking for was a special helper, a helper fit to help him to accomplish God's work. Man was looking for the best helper who would best help him to do God's work in such a way that God would be most satisfied.

B. MAN'S STANDARD FOR A HELPER FIT

The fact that man did not just accept anything that was brought to him by the Lord God shows that he clearly unders-tood the fact that God was not forcing things on him. It further shows the fact that he knew what he was looking for and, the-refore, was prepared to wait until he found what he wanted. He was more or less saying that although he needed a helper, he would rather stay without a helper than have just any helper. He understood the full implications of having a helper. He knew that the helper he accepted would influence him in a most pro-found way, and that he could succeed or fail in his life's goal, de-pending on who that helper was.

He, therefore, had his standard against which he weighed all the creature that the Lord brought to him. The helper fit had to :

- Be capable of entering into the fullest fellowship with-God.
- Be capable of entering into the fullest fellowship with himself.
- Be capable of understanding in full measure the work that God had called him to do for Him.

- Be prepared to commit all of herself to that work and, thereby, make it her life's goal to help him to accomplish that work.

He was prepared to choose only the one who could be the best in each of these spheres. He was determined not to settle for mediocrity when God was prepared to give him the best.

He also ensured that he was what he should be. Therefore, in looking for a helper fit he, too, ensured that he would be to her a helper fit. Therefore man had to :

- Labour to enter into the fullest fellowship with God and maintain it.
- Be prepared to let all of himself go, so he could enter into the fullest fellowship with his partner.
- Labour to understand in full measure the work that God had for him to do.
- Commit himself without reservation to that work and make it his life's goal to ensure that that work was done to the best satisfaction of God.

So marriage in God's purpose required two helpers fit to help each other to accomplish the work of God. Marriage is the union of two helpers fit to accomplish God's work.

Man was created fit. He possessed God's life; he was in vital fellowship with God. He was totally committed to the Lord. He was given work by God and he understood what that work was. He was committed to that work. In addition, he had a capacity to give himself away completely and to build the partner into all that God wanted.

Being himself fit, the only problem now was the search for and the acquisition of a helper fit. The animals, birds, etc., could not be man's helper fit. This is obvious because of the following reasons:

First of all, these creatures did not have God's nature. They could, therefore, not enter into vital fellowship with God. They could not discern the needs of God and respond freely to these.

Secondly, not having God's nature that was in man, they could not enter into full fellowship with man. They could not share man's ambitions and purposes.

Thirdly, they could not understand God's work and could not consciously commit themselves to it.

Fourthly, they had no overriding purpose which man could help them to accomplish. These failures on the part of the animals and birds eliminated them from any possibility that any one of them could become a helper fit for the man.

C. GOD SECURES A HELPER FIT

God never gives up any of His purposes, regardless of how much time it takes and how difficult the task is. He will spare nothing in order to bring His ordained purpose to pass. With regard to the finding of a helper fit for man, He decided to carry out a surgical operation. He caused a deep sleep to fall upon the man and, while he slept, He took out one of his ribs and made it into a woman.

The woman thus came out of the man. She, therefore, had all

that the man had. She had:

- God's nature.
- A capacity for very deep fellowship with God.
- A capacity for a very profound relationship with man.
- Knowledge of God's work and a willingness to do it God's way and for God's purpose.

She was a compatible partner. She was a helper fit.

D. MAN CHOOSES THE WOMAN

After God had made the woman, He brought her to Adam just as He had brought the other creatures. He did not woo Adam into accepting her. He did not suggest it to him. Immediately when Adam saw her he spoke out, *"This at last is bone of my bones and flesh of my flesh; she shall be called Woman because she was taken out of Man"* (Genesis 2:23). When Adam saw the woman, he immediately chose her to be his. There was no compulsion. He was free to give her a name and to treat her as he had treated all the other creatures that God had brought to him. Instead, he shouted for joy. He said, "This at last..." Yes, "at last!"

The search had taken much time. She was not easy to come by, but at last she was found. He accepted her fully and with total joy. He made her his choice. Had he not made her his choice, God would have gone ahead to seek someone who would be accepted by him as his perfect choice. Adam brought the process of seeking for a helper fit for him to an end when he saw in the woman all that he wanted. She was his helper fit! God had made her. Man chose her for himself and the matter was settled.

With the choice made, man could then enter into the marriage relationship with his wife. In the purpose of God, marriage comes after the choosing has taken place. The Bible says, *"The-*

refore a man leaves his father and his mother and cleaves to his wife, and they become one flesh" (Genesis 2.24).

The question arises: When can a man leave his father and his mother and cleave to his wife, and the two become one flesh? The Bible's answer is that a man may leave his father and his mother and cleave to his wife, and the two of them become one flesh when the man has satisfied the following conditions:

1. He has received God's nature through the new birth.
2. He has committed himself to a vital relationship with God in deepest union.
3. He has seen God's work for him.
4. He is totally committed to that work.
5. He has the approval from God that he needs a helper fit for that Work.
6. He is committed to making himself one that can be helped.
7. He has seen and chosen the helper fit for himself whom God has for him.

And the woman in turn has:

1. Received God's nature through the new birth,
2. Committed herself to a vital relationship with God in deepest union,
3. Seen a man called by God to do God's work,
4. Received from God that that man needs a helper fit for the work,
5. Received from God that she is that helper fit for the man,
6. Been chosen by the man to be his helper fit,
7. Chosen the man who has chosen her.

Until these crucial matters are settled, no two people may be involved in any sexual relationship. To do so would be to court the disfavour of God.

E. WHEN A MAN CHOOSES AND A WOMAN ACCEPTS TO BE CHOSEN

When a man chooses a woman he must ask himself the following question:

"Is this woman the best suited to help me to accomplish all of the work that God has called me to do for Him?"

If she is not, she should be left alone. She is not God's choice for you. You must not choose her.

Before a woman accepts a man, she must ask herself the following question:

"Is this man totally committed to the will of God so that in becoming his helper, I shall be totally satisfying the heart of God?"

If the man is totally committed to the will of God, then a commitment to help him will be a commitment to the total will of God. If the man is divided at heart, then a commitment to become his wife will be a commitment to divided loyalty. If the man is purposeless, then a commitment to him will be a commitment to advance purposelessness, for you will help him to accomplish purposelessness.

CHAPTER 5

God's purpose for a wife

We have said that God had work for man to do, and that the purpose of giving him a wife was so that she could be his helper fit to help him to do his God-given task.

The question then arises as to man's special responsibility to the wife. While she is to help him to accomplish his God-given task, what must he do for her? The Bible puts this out by inference. In talking about Christ and His bride, the church, the Bible says, *"Husbands, love your wives, as Christ loved the church and gave himself up for her, that He might sanctify her, having cleansed her by the washing of water with the word, that he might present the church to himself in splendour, without spot or wrinkle or any such thing, that she might be holy and without blemish"* (Ephesians 5:25-27). Husbands have one supreme responsibility to their wives. It is that they should labour, strive and work so that they may, on the Day of Judgement, present their wives to Christ in splendour

without spot,
without wrinkle,
without blemish.

Without spot means that she should be without sin. Without wrinkle means that she should maintain her first love for the Lord Jesus. Without blemish means that the fruit of the Spirit should mature in her in such a way that she will present the full spectrum of the character of Christ.

On that day, God wants wives presented to Christ by their husbands in all the splendour of Christ. In the marriage relationship then, a man has this as the one thing towards which to direct all his attention as far as his wife is concerned. He is not to ask, "Has she done this or that for me? Has she gone here or there for me?" He is to ask himself, "What have I done to ensure that she is growing in the splendour of the Lord Jesus? What spots, wrinkles and blemishes are there on her that I have to labour to ensure that they are removed?"

According to God's purpose, a man is to set himself life-long goals, yearly goals, monthly goals, weekly goals and daily goals on how to ensure that his wife grows in the splendour of the Lord Jesus. He is to ask himself at the end of each day, "Have I helped her today to grow in splendour?" If a man fails to prepare his wife in such a way that he will present her to the Lord in splendour, then he has failed as far as his marriage is concerned. Every woman has a God-given right to expect her husband to do all that can be done at any cost to ensure that she grows in the splendour of the Lord.

With this in view, two serious questions arise about the choice of a life partner. From the woman's point of view, she must seriously ask herself about anyone who wants to be married to her, "Is this the man who will best be able to labour and do all that must be done for me so that on that day I am presented to the Lord with as much glory as possible?" She must not settle for anything less than the best. From the man's point of view, he must ask one question: "Is this the woman whom I will be able to present to the Lord Jesus in the fullest glory possible, after putting in all that is possible?"

The woman will look, in the man, for the potential to present her to the Lord in splendour. The man will look, in the woman, for potential for growth in splendour and for the capacity to co-operate with him in his task of labouring to ensure that she is presented to the Lord in splendour.

This means that the man must choose the woman and the wo-man must choose the man. Each is responsible for his choice.

God's purpose for a wife is that she be presented to Christ in splendour on the last day. All husbands must labour to accom-plish that goal.

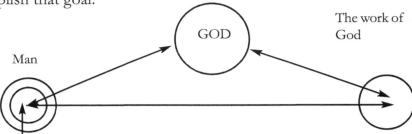

In the purposes of God, the marriage is the union between two people who are in a vital communion with God, having received God's nature through Lord Jésus-Christ. Each of the parts has in mind God's work and committed to it in a absolute way, being ready to carry it out accor-ding to the ways of God and for the glory of God. Each of the partners sees in the other one, that or the one who could best help him to carry to achieve this purpose. In this way, God and his work are the reasons which lead to the marriage, and God remains the center of this marriage. The marriage thus becomes a commitment for the glory of God and not just an activity for the pleasure of the man or the woman.

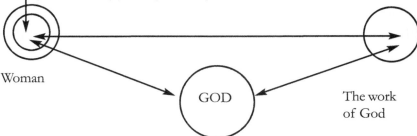

Fig. 5 : The two parties who may enter into a marriage that will satisfy God.

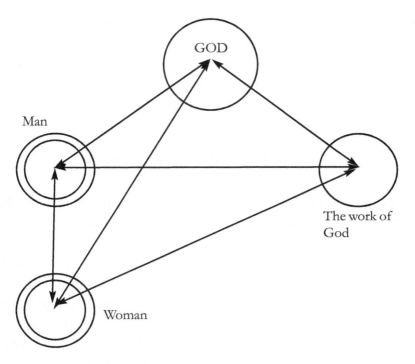

Fig. 6 : God's original purpose for marriage.

A. MARRIAGE IS NOT A MUST

God has not called all men and women whom He has created into the married life.

There are men who are rightly related to God, who have received God's special work for their lives, and who are meant to do that work alone without the help of a partner. God has no helper fit for them. He Himself is their helper fit. If such men then go out and get married, they will have a marriage that fails because it was not in the purpose of God.

The same thing applies to women. There are women whom

God does not intend to be married and help some man to do His work. God intends them to help Him. He is the One they are to help. Should such women then go ahead and marry, the marriage will not work because that marriage was never in God's original purpose for their lives.

B. A PRIMARY QUESTION

Because God has not called all people into marriage, the first thing that each man and each woman should do is to find out from God if He has marriage as part of His plan for them. They should not go ahead to seek a life partner unless they have found out clearly before God that He intends them to be married. There are many people who would have been happier had they not been married and, more so, there are many people who have frustrated God's great purpose for their lives by being married, whereas God had meant them to be single.

Each person must surrender totally to God and find out what God wants. All surrendered people will eventually find out that God's will for them, be it the single life or the married life, is the best for them. Do not misunderstand me. I am not saying that marriage is bad. Far from it; for it was ordained by God and the Bible says that he who finds a wife finds a good thing and obtains favour from the Lord (Proverbs 18:22), and that two are better than one (Ecclesiastes 4:9). We can even include Deuteronomy 32:30 where the Bible talks of the possibility of one chasing one thousand and two putting ten thousand to flight. This could also include the two in a marriage relationship.

Although marriage is good and it is God's general purpose for the human race, it is not necessarily God's perfect will for every man or woman. The Lord Jesus Himself never married. The apostles who were called unmarried remained so, the burden of the ministry giving them no room for the cares of marriage. The Lord Jesus said, *"For there are eunuchs who have been made eunuchs by men, and there are eunuchs who have made themselves eunuchs for the sake of the kingdom of heaven. He who is able to receive this, let him receive it"* (Matthew 19:12).

So there will be people prevented by the situations of life from being married; they are made eunuchs by man. (Such people exist, both believers and unbelievers). There will be others who, on their own, and not because it is imposed on them by some man or system, decide that they will stay single so as to put all of themselves into the work of the Lord and not to be sidetracked by the cares of a wife and children which marriage necessarily brings.

So be surrendered. God will not force you to be single. However, if He calls you into the single life because of the work He has for you, and you willingly and gladly accept that call, you will be blessed.

So it is good to settle this question before you start to look for a possible partner.

MARRIAGE AS MAN HAS MADE IT

CHAPTER 6

Man's distorted purpose for marriage

Although God created man for Himself and put His nature within man, man rebelled against God and has since been living in rebellion and independence. God's nature is no longer central to man and the relationship between God and man is no longer vital. In addition to this, man has put God's purpose and God's work aside, and is carrying out his own purpose and his own work. Even when he does the work of God, it is for God's glory but also for his personal glory, or for the glory of something he likes.

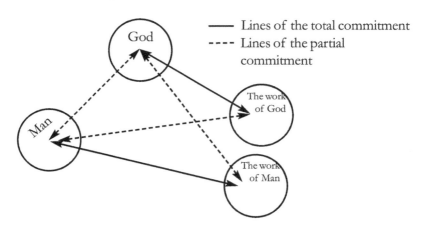

Fig. 7 : *The Spirit of God no longer dwells in rebellious man. God has no deep fellowship with man. Man is not fully concerned with doing God's work for God's glory. Rather, he is taken up with doing his own work for his own glory.*

Rebellious man, filled with sin, has made himself the centre of life. He does everything for one selfish reason or the other. Even his generosity is rooted in the desire for praise. He wants to be the centre of reference, wants people to bow down to his ideas and opinions and to do what he wants. Those who do not see with him nor worship him, he considers as terrible people.

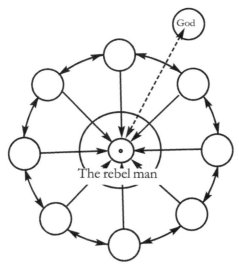

Fig. 8: *Rebellious man has made himself the centre of life and gathered around himself people who will worship and approve of his thoughts and actions. He is self-centred. God is far away and His influence is rejected except when man is in need.*

Rebellious man, in his sin, is not filled with the Spirit of God. He is filled with sin. This sin manifests itself in sins which include:

1. Fornication.
2. Adultery.
3. Masturbation.
4. Impure thoughts.
5. Immoral thoughts.
6. Reading of dirty books and magazines.

7. Seeing dirty films.

8. Going to night clubs and immoral places.

9. Lying.

10. Exaggerations.

11. Anger.

12. Wrath.

13. Wickedness.

14. Malice.

15. Abortion.

16. Homosexuality.

17. Lesbianism.

18. Petting.

19. Bitterness.

20. Strife.

21. An unforgiving attitude.

22. Selfishness.

23. Covetousness.

24. Greed.

25. Jealousy.

26. Quarrelling.

27. Fighting.

28. Gossip.

29. Slander.

30. Mocking God.

31. Mocking true believers.

32. Persecution of believers.

33. Stealing.

34. Cheating.

35. Corruption.

36. Bribery.

37. Pride.

38. Haughtiness.

39. Cowardice.
40. Murder.
41. Favouritism.
42. Nepotism.
43. Laziness.
44. Indiscipline.
45. Harshness.
46. Cruelty.
47. Faithlessness.
48. Mercilessness.
49. Revengefulness.
50. Disobedience to parents.
51. Disobedience to other authority.
52. Envy.
53. Idleness.
54. Gluttony.
55. Drunkenness.
56. Sorcery.
57. Magic.
58. Palmistry.
59. Witchcraft.
60. Grumbling.
61. Lovelessness.
62. Carelessness.
63. Stinginess.
64. Rudeness.
65. Vanity.
66. Egotism.
67. Self-righteousness.
68. Self-justification.
69. Self-advertisement.
70. Self-praise.

Sinful man in his sinful state wants a wife for selfish reasons. These reasons may include the following:

He wants a woman who will:

- satisfy his sexual desires legitimately,
- bear him children,
- cook his food,
- take care of his house,
- take care of his parents,
- improve his financial position,
- enable him to pay less taxes,
- enable him to get the job he desires,
- wash his clothes,
- advance his tribe,
- win him the admiration of others.

At the centre of it all is what he wants. There is often no thought about what she wants. She is just one of the many people who should revolve around him.

Sinful woman, in her rebellion against God, wants someone who will also revolve around her. She wants someone whom she can use to accomplish her selfish ends.

She wants a man who will:
- satisfy her sexual desires legitimately,
- give her legal children,
- provide her with a regular source of income,
- provide for her endless material needs,
- win her the respect of others,

- provide her with security,
- satisfy her desire to be owned,
- take away her loneliness,
- take care of her family,
- worship her and make her feel like a queen,
- advance her education or career.

Mutual Exploitation

Sinful man and sinful woman are both self-centred. Since God's work has been replaced by man's work and God has been replaced by the 'self', each thinks of what he/she can get out of the marriage deal. Therefore, in considering the choice of a life partner, no one asks what he or she has to give. The emphasis is on an analysis of the benefits that could be gotten out of it. One girl told me, "I have always hated men, but I did not want to have illegitimate children and, so, I got married." A man told me, "Women are to be used. They are not to be taken seriously. Use them. If you don't use them, they will use you." Another man said, "Be sure that you never love a woman. If you ever did, she would know it and from that day she would rule you."

Because of their separation from God, they consciously or unconsciously choose their life partners for selfish reasons. One man wants the best cook. Another wants the one who will produce the most beautiful children. Another wants the woman who will best fit into his tribal setting and, so, he chooses on the basis of the tribe. Another one chooses on the basis of wealth and, so, he looks for a woman who comes from a rich family and whose relatives have much to give in terms of wealth. Others marry into families that will advance their political careers. Others marry for purely sexual reasons. One man said, "I am tired of running from one woman to another without guarantee each night. I must have my own woman at home so that my night trips can be reduced." So it is what he can get out of her. He is bent on exploiting her. His choices are rooted in his desire to exploit. One man once said, "I have spent my life sampling women – the black, the brown, the tall, the short, the slim and the fat. I have used all types and I have found out that they are all ultimately the same."

Because women are also equally separated from God, they do not approach the subject from God's point of view. They are preoccupied with their own desires. They look for a man who can be used as an instrument of security. Or they look for a man who can be used as an instrument to supply money. They, therefore, try to get the richest man that they can get. Or they want a man who can improve on the financial possibilities of their parents and relatives. They will, therefore, prefer a rich old man to a young man who is just trying to start out in life. Or they may choose someone who will satisfy their vain desires for luxurious housing, clothing, jewelry, cars, hotels, etc., regardless of what he looks like, what he knows, or what he lives for. The only thing that matters is what they can get out of him. Others want to be accepted by a society that looks down on the unmarried, and so they get attached to someone at any cost. The dominant thing in their thinking is, "Let me at least bear the title 'Mrs.'"

No thought for the partner

Because sinful man has rebelled against God and is totally self-centred in his attitude toward life, his thoughts about a possible life partner never dwell on: "What do I have to offer to my partner? What will I take with me into marriage? What blessings will

I bring to her? Will I be able to satisfy her in the depth of her being?" Because of self-centredness, these serious questions are never asked or, if they are asked, they are asked in passing and no one ever takes time to work out the answers. This means that many people do not prepare seriously for the needs of the other party. Many never ask if they are being fair to the other party.

A man who has had sexual experiences with a multitude of women will want to a marry a virgin without asking himself about her own needs to marry a virgin man, so that both of them may start out together in a marriage to learn all that is involved in sex. A man who has made many girls pregnant will refuse to be married to a girl who has once committed an abortion, without thinking of his own acts. A man who has left strings of bastards here and there will still say, "I do not want to marry any girl who has had a child with someone else." A forty-five year old man will say, "I do not want to marry a girl over-matured through struggling to be educated. I want a fresh young girl of eighteen," etc. So, all through, men only think of their needs, of what they can get out of women. Not once do they think about the woman's needs, about what they have to offer the woman and whether or not the woman will find fulfilment.

But it is not only men who are selfish in their choices. Women are equally thoughtless of men. It is I, I, I. For example, a girl could give her body to ten, twenty, thirty or forty men. She could allow herself to be used left and right. She could commit abortion after abortion. She could suffer one heart-break after another and end up being full of bitterness, and then she would look for someone on whom to deposit the remains of her life, that is, more or less like the remains of a car that has been involved in many serious accidents. Meanwhile, she may pretend and tell the man, "You are the first man in my life!" She might have had venereal diseases many times and fears that she may never have children, but she would not tell all this to the man. Rather she would grab him, plan a wedding in which she wears white and a veil, and pretend to be a virgin indeed. Others just go into marriage to use men to solve their problems. One woman told another, "I do not love this man, but I must have him. He is my security against the hardships of old age." Others allow a different man to make them pregnant but, because the one who made them pregnant is not well-to-do, they trap another man who is socially better placed into a relationship with them and then pretend that he is the father of their baby. Others allow themselves to be made pregnant by a married man whom they cannot marry and then make some young unmarried man the scapegoat for their pregnancy and insist that he should marry them. Others make promises to men, "I will marry you. I will be faithful to you." But no sooner have they seen another man they prefer, than these promises disappear as if they had never been made. Others say, "Darling, you can count on me till the sun dries up the sea. Until then, I will always be devoted to you." And while the world's seas remain filled with water, they change their minds many times over.

In all these choices and actions, there is no thought for the partner. All thinking is centred on the self. While the man thinks of using the woman, the woman thinks of using the man.

Fig. 9
The relationship is a conscious or unconscious attempt to exploit the other party. The man wants to use the woman to satisfy his own desires, and the woman also wants to use the man to satisfy her own desires. Such a relationship is doomed to fail because each party will eventually find out that it is being used, or that the partner cannot be exploited to the extent that he/she thought.

Two self-centred people may begin by being very nice to each other. They may not know that they are self-centred. They may not know this because they are separated from God by their sin, they cannot help being self-centred. So they begin by being nice and good to each other. They may be excited about each other. Maybe they even sacrificed for each other, but at their best their sacrifices are tinted with germ of the self-life. It is, "I will do this to her so that she may love me more. I will treat her this well so that she may keep me in her heart always. I must be this or that to her so that she will have no thoughts about any other man but me." Do you see that these actions may be good, but the motives are selfish? Do you notice that it is all "I... for me?" Yes, all the motives of sinners are self-centred to varying degrees. This self-centredness may not be manifest, but it is there like a sleeping giant. The other party may think, "Oh, how she loves me! Oh, how she is prepared to sacrifice for me! Oh, how humble she is! Oh, how thoughtless of her own needs she is!" Etc. Let him wait until they are married and then the giant of the self in her will wake up from its sleep, and he will have it. One man said to me, "I courted and married a young tender girl. Two years after marriage, I have a full grown lioness in my house and, poor me, I am finished." A woman said to me, "When we were courting each other my fiancé was so tender and sweet. He would have gladly done anything to make me happy. He gave me everything that I wanted and went with me to every place I wanted to go. Afterwards, we got married. I thought it was going to be an unending honeymoon. But, Oh! How he has changed! He is a totally different man from the boy who courted me and promised to make my life happy. He is hard, very hard. I never hear one soft word from his lips. He beats me and does not want to see me. He is happy away from me, but when he is with me he is withdrawn and angry. I never thought that something that began so well could end so badly." Yes, it began very well. The lion of the "self" in him was asleep and she thought it was absent. He has not changed. He is just being himself – fully himself. He does not need to pretend anymore. He pretended in order to capture her. Why should he pretend any longer?

As we said earlier, even the most handsome, gentle, educated man without Christ is a sinner. He may be

a gentle liar,
a handsome hypocrite,
an educated egotist.

He may be sincere, but sincerely self-centred,
sincerely merciless,
sincerely wicked,
sincerely haughty,
sincerely rude.

He may have good intentions, but these good intentions are not strong enough to change him from his true nature, which

may include adultery,
    greed,
    bitterness,
    lovelessness.

As for her, she may be tall, slim, well-dressed and warm, but she may be a tall, slim and well-dressed
    abortionist,
    wicked woman,
    hard-hearted person,
    lover of money,
    lover of vanity,
    self-centred person,
    whose only concern may be herself, her family, her future.
To her, the man is only a means to an end.

Do you blame her?

The choices of all rebels are wrong

It is quite evident that many people, while continuing in their sin and rebellion against God, have gone ahead and made choices of life partners. We say emphatically that all their choices are wrong. There are many obvious reasons for this assertion.

First of all, all sinners are wrong. They are wrong beings. The Bible says, "*None is righteous, no, not one; no one understands, no one seeks for God. All have turned aside, together they have gone wrong; no one does good, not even one. Their throat is an open grave, they use their tongues to deceive. The venom of asps is under their lips. Their mouth is full of curses and bitterness. Their feet are swift to shed blood, in their paths are ruin and misery, and the way of peace they do not know. There is no fear of God before their eyes*" (Romans 3:10-18)

"*The fool says in his heart, 'There is no God.' They are corrupt, they do abominable deeds, there is none that does good. The Lord looks down from heaven upon the children of men, to see if there are any that act wisely, that seek after God. They have all gone astray, they are all alike corrupt; there is none that does good, no, not one*" (Psalm 14:1-3)

All sinners are also selfish. They are filled with themselves. Can a wrong being make a right choice? No! Can a self-centred being make a choice that is totally free of selfishness? No. So, because the sinner is wrong, because he is separated from God who is the Source of all wisdom, because he is full of himself, all his choices must be wrong. On a surface view, the choice may seem right, but it is not right. It can't be right. All the choices of rebels are wrong.

The second reason why the choices of all sinners are wrong has to do with the very purpose of marriage. Marriage was ordained by God so that a person who is rightly related to Him and has found out His purpose for him, should have a helper fit to help him to do God's work. The rebel is separated from God. The rebel is committed to the rebel's work, and the choice of the rebel has nothing to do with God's purpose. How can such a choice be right? The person choosing is wrong, the person being chosen is wrong, and the motive for choosing is wrong. All is wrong. God looks at all the choices of people who are in rebellion against Him as tragic disorders.

The third reason why the choices of sinners are wrong is that the man never prepares his wife in order that he may present her to Christ in splendour. He instead tries to prepare her so as to present her to himself in his glory. So he labours to make her into something he can use. She, in turn, does the same thing, and the results are obvious – divorce, quarrels, bitterness, etc.

The fourth reason why the choices of rebels are wrong is that these choices lead to wrong marriages, and the product of such marriages bear clear witness to what the man and the woman are. Whether something is right or wrong can also be tested by what it produces. Read the following example:

"Max Jules, the atheist, lived a godless life. He married an ungodly woman. From that union the following were produced:
- 310 who died as paupers.
- 150 were criminals.
- 7 were murderers.

- 100 were drunkards.
- More than half of the women were prostitutes.
- His 540 known descendants cost the United States government 1,250,000 dollars." (That is about 600,000,000 CFA francs).

"Jonathan Edward (a leading preacher of the Gospel of Jesus Christ) lived at the same time as the atheist Max Jules. He married a godly woman. An investigation was made of his 1394 known descendants :
- 13 became college presidents (Chancellors or Vice-chancellors).
- 65 became college professors (University lecturers).
- 3 became United States senators.
- 30 became judges.
- 100 became lawyers.
- 60 became medical doctors.
- 75 became army and navy officers.
- 100 became preachers and missionaries.
- 60 became authors of prominence.
- 1 became a Vice-President of the United States of America.
- 80 became public officers in other capacities.
- 295 became University graduates among whom were: State governors.
- United States representatives to foreign countries.

None of his descendants cost the United States government a cent." (Quoted from the book, "Meat For Men" by L. Ravenhill.)
Do you want to continue in your sin and become a liability to

your descendants for many generations? The Lord God said, *"I the Lord your God am a jealous God, visiting the iniquity of the fathers upon the children to the third and the fourth generation of those who hate me, but showing steadfast love to thousands of those who love me and keep my commandments"* (Exodus 20:5-6).

Do you want to bring a curse on your children, grand children, great-grandchildren, etc., or do you want to be a blessing for them? If you continue in sin, you will bring judgement on yourself and woe on them. You dare not do that.

A NEW HUMANITY IS A MUST

We have seen that man and woman are distorted because of their rebellion against God. We have also seen that such people will look at the choice of a life partner in terms of what they can get out of it. Their one concern is what the partner is and what he/she has. They will see things in the partners that they want and possibly marry them in order to have those things. Unfortunately, they will discover that their partners also married them so as to get something out of them. So the struggle begins with each trying to get out as much as possible, and each trying to give away as little as possible. This leads to failure. The average marriage is a failure. Many marriages end in divorce and many more continue, even though the relationship is totally or partially broken. Many continue as married, but in their hearts the divorce has already taken place.

The problem in the relationship is not the other partner. The problem is each partner. Both partners are bound by the devil. They are his servants. They are separated from God. They are separated from God's purpose. They have substituted God's purpose for marriage by their own purpose, and things can never work. The problem is not with marriage. The problem is not with mistakes made in choosing. The problem is more fundamental. There is a problem with every man and every woman who is born into the world. Each one is a wrong being that needs to be put right. The distorted rebel needs, first of all, to be changed. Secondly, the new person produced by this change must seek God's purpose for his life. Thirdly, that person must then choose a life partner who will help him to accomplish God's purpose for him.

Happiness in marriage can never come directly. It must come indirectly. It must come from a combined commitment to know

God and to serve Him. Those who seek happiness directly will miss it. Those who seek God and serve Him will find that happiness is theirs.

This means that something must happen to each human being before there can be the right choice. The man must be right. The woman must be right. Then the right man must choose the right woman.

But all men and women are distorted through sin and rebellion against God. No one in that condition can be right, and no one in that condition can choose rightly. The first thing then is the change of the wrong man and woman into the right man and woman before God. There must be a new humanity out of the old humanity.

CHAPTER 8

The genesis of the old humanity

When God created Adam and put His nature within him, He commanded him to obey. The first man and the first woman were to live in harmony with each other as they obeyed God. Unfortunately, they disobeyed God and their relationship with God was broken. They were no longer at home in God's presence, and there was discord between them. The man even blamed God for giving him a wife, and announced that their disobedience was due to her. He excused himself and blamed the woman. The woman also excused herself and blamed the serpent. Each shifted the blame to the other. Adam talked about her in distant terms. She was no longer close to him. They had both left God's work aside and, at the suggestion of the serpent, they were doing Satan's work. Three things happened when they sinned :

1. Their relationship with God was broken.
2. Their relationship with God's work was broken, and they did the devil's work.
3. Their relationship with each other was broken.

They become the beginning of humanity that is
separated from God,
separated from God's work,
separated from each other.

God's nature that was put into them was distorted, broken and twisted. That humanity is the old humanity. It is made up of people bound by sin and self. It is made of people who are out of fellowship with God and who are preoccupied with their own work.

God, in His wondrous love, has not abandoned man to his deserved doom. God went out of His way to create a new humanity out of the old humanity.

THE DEATH OF CHRIST ON THE CROSS

The old humanity sold itself to Satan and became his children. The Bible says that Satan has children. The Lord Jesus, in talking to Jewish religious leaders, referred to them as the children of the devil. He said, *"You are of your father the devil, and your will is to do your father's desires. He was a murderer from the beginning, and has nothing to do with the truth, because there is no truth in him. When he lies, he speaks according to his own nature, for he is a liar and the father of lies"* (John 8:44). The devil is the father of lies. He is the father of liars. All who lie are the devil's children. They do his will and his will is to fill the world with lies. Do you lie? It may be in a small way or in a big way. The degree of lying does not matter. Whenever a lie comes forth, it comes out of a person who is a child of the devil. In this way it is very easy to tell who is a child of the devil. You see, these people were religious leaders. They were also liars. They were unmistakably the children of the devil. In another occasion someone wanted to turn from sin unto the Lord Jesus Christ. There was a magician who knew that this transfer from Satan to Jesus would cause him to lose a client and he tried to disturb the man from coming to Christ. Paul addressed the magician in the following words, *"You son of the devil, you enemy of all righteousness, full of deceit*

and villainy, will you not stop making crooked the straight paths of the Lord?" (Acts 13:10). The magician was called
a son of the devil,
an enemy of all righteousness,
full of deceit,
full of villainy.

All magicians are sons of the devil.
All who prevent people from turning to Christ are sons of the devil.
All deceitful people are sons of the devil.
All villains are sons of the devil.
All sinners are sons of the devil.
All thieves are sons of the devil.
All fornicators are sons of the devil.
All adulterers are sons of the devil.
All who give bribes are sons of the devil.
All who receive bribes are sons of the devil.
All who commit abortion are sons of the devil.
All hypocrites are sons of the devil.
All who are lazy are sons of the devil.
All who are wicked are sons of the devil.
All who are proud,
  haughty,
  arrogant,
  boastful or despise others, etc.,
are sons of the devil.

All who carry out any of Satan's work are sons of the devil.
You who still enjoy one sin or the other, who live in active, partial or passive rebellion against God are a son of the devil !

CHAPTER 9

The destiny of the old humanity

The devil's children will share the devil's home eternally

The devil has a home and he will be sent there in the end. The Bible says, *"And the devil who had deceived them was thrown into the lake of fire and sulphur where the beast and the false prophet were, and they will be tormented day and night for ever and ever"* (Revelation 20:10).

"He who conquers shall have this heritage, and I will be his God and he shall be my son. But as for the cowardly, the faithless, the polluted, as for murderers, fornicators, sorcerers, idolaters, and all liars, their lot shall be in the lake that burns with fire and sulphur, which is the second death" (Revelation 21:7-8).

"And I saw the dead, great and small, standing before the throne, and books were opened. Also another book was opened, which is the book of life. And the dead were judged by what was written in the books, by what they had done. And the sea gave up the dead in it, Death and Hades gave up the dead in them, and all were judged by what they had done. Then Death and Hades were thrown into the lake of fire. This is the second death, the lake of fire; and if anyone's name was not found written in the book of life, he was thrown into the lake of fire" (Revelation 20:12-15).

You know for certain that you are a rebel. You are a sinner. You commit sin. You are bound by sin. You may choose a life partner or you may not choose one. You may be married or single. You may be rich or poor. You may be educated or uneducated. You may have a big job or no job at all. One thing, however, is certain. If you remain in your present condition of sin, as a child of the devil, you will go to the lake of fire. God must punish you for your rebellion. He will certainly punish you because of your sin. It does not matter whether you have sinned to a small extent or to a great extent. The quantity of sin is of no consequence. Even if there is only one sin, you are a sinner and will be thrown into the lake of fire. You can look at it this way: If a man steals ten million francs and another steals ten francs, what have they done? They have stolen different amounts of money, but they are both thieves and they will be punished as thieves. All sinners – small and great – will be thrown into the lake of fire. You may want to look at it in a different way: If a mango tree produces ten thousand mango fruits, it is a mango tree. Is it not? If, on the other hand, another mango tree produces only ten mangoes, or even just one mango, or even no mango at all, does it cease to be a mango tree? Of course not; it remains a mango tree, regardless of how many mangoes it produces. A sinner is a rebel. His rebellion may bear little or no fruit. Nevertheless, the rebellion is there, and God will punish the sinner by throwing him into the lake of fire.

You may tell me that you do not believe in the existence of hell. You may say that God is too loving to punish sinners forever. You may even say that there is no God. You may say that there is no life after death. You may say that when you die that will be the end, but do you realize that in the passage above (Revelation 20:12-15) it is the dead, great and small, that stand before the throne of God to be judged and then sentenced to the second death in the lake of fire? So death will not end your problems. You will be judged. You must be judged. If you care to do so, you can rationalize God's truth as you like. You can choose to hide yourself in the deception that there will be no hell. However, one day when you will stand before Jesus Christ - the great Judge, and are sentenced to the lake of fire forever, you will be a great believer in Christ on that day, but it will be too late. You will believe very fervently in the existence of hell as you kiss the flames and "enjoy" the suffocating odours of the changing sulphur gases. You will believe but it will be too late. Now is the time to do something about your rebellion.

CHAPTER 10

The new humanity - 1 :
The treasure of great price

The Lord Jesus told a parable in the Bible which went as follows:

"The kingdom of heaven is like treasure hidden in a field, which a man found and covered up; then in his joy he goes and sells all that he has and buys that field" (Matthew 13:44).

Who is the man in this parable and what is the treasure? The man in the parable is the Lord Jesus Christ, the Son of God. The treasure is the sinner, created in God's image, but lost through rebellion and bound by sin and on the way to eternal destruction in the lake of fire. The Lord Jesus sat on the throne of glory and He saw the sinner in his lost condition. The Lord then made the sinner a treasure of great price and took seven steps down into total degradation, giving everything away so that He might purchase the sinner back to Himself.

The Bible says: *"Have this mind among yourselves, which is yours in Jesus Christ, who, though he was in the form of God, did not count equality with God a thing to be grasped, but emptied himself, taking the form of a servant, being born in the likeness of men. And being found in human form he humbled himself and became obedient unto death, even death on a cross"* (Philippians 2:5-8). What were the seven steps that the Lord Jesus took into total degradation so that He might purchase you, the sinner and the treasure of great price?

STEP ONE : HE EMPTIED HIMSELF

Jesus was God. He was in the form of God. He was called, *"Wonderful Counsellor, Mighty God, Everlasting Father, Prince of Peace"* (Isaiah 9:6). Being therefore the Mighty God, the Everlasting Father, He was in every way God. He could have said, "I am God, I will remain God and be equal to God." If He had thought and acted that way, He would have been right. He would have remained in heaven. Man would have been lost and the Lord would not have purchased the treasure of great price – the sinner. However, He took the first step into degradation. He decided to cross that eternal gap that separates God from all that is not God. It is not possible for man to fully understand what it must have cost Him to move from being God to being someone else other than God. It suffices to say that He emptied Himself of being God. The treasure cost Him that much.

STEP TWO : HE COULD HAVE BECOME AN ANGEL

Jesus could have said, "I will give up My form as God. I will become 'not God' but in that condition I must choose the form of the created being that is most supernatural. I will become an angel or some such heavenly creature." Had the Lord thought that way, He would have had a right to His thoughts and actions. He could have become an angel. However, in coming as low as angels, He would have been capable of purchasing creatures that were like angels and above that. He would have left man, the sinner, unpurchased.

STEP THREE : HE BECAME A MAN

Jesus Christ went below the form of angels. He actually became a man. He accepted to be born in the likeness of man. He took upon Himself the total humanity of man except the fallen nature. This was a most risky affair. When God the Son took upon Himself the form of man, He took a most serious step. If, as a man, He had sinned, then God the Son would have sinned. It would then have become impossible for Him to return to the Godhead. You would then have had the Godhead consisting only of God the Father and God the Holy Spirit. Now, the Godhead cannot continue without the Son. We conclude that the entire Godhead stood in jeopardy when Jesus took the form of man. This brings out one thing very clearly, and it is: The entire Godhead paid the price for the purchase of that treasure called sinful man. It was not just the affair of the Son alone. God the Father and God the Holy Spirit were equally involved, and they paid for it at the risk of their very existence. The Bible says, *"God was in Christ reconciling the world to himself"* (2 Corinthians 5:19). So God paid the price for the purchase of the sinner.

STEP FOUR : HE DID NOT BECOME
AN IMPORTANT MAN

The Lord Jesus could have said, "I will go and become a man; but as a man, I must become an important man." He could have said, "Let there be some difference at least. Let me receive some honour even though I am a man." He could have opted to become a king, a president, or such a great man. If He had opted for that, and He could have opted for that, He could have saved only people who were of that standing. His salvation would have been limited to important sinners. However, Jesus did not choose to become an important man. He opted for something lower.

STEP FIVE : HE HUMBLED HIMSELF AND BECAME A SLAVE

The lowest state of human life is that of a slave. He has no rights whatsoever. He can be sold, resold, or killed at his master's will. He owns nothing and expects nothing for himself. Jesus humbled Himself and did not become an important human being; not a free human being of middle estate; not a free human being of low estate; He became a slave. We shall never be able to understand the degree of humiliation that was involved for Him until we meet Him face to face. When that day does come, and we see Him as He is indeed and understand how low He came, we shall worship Him more unreservedly and be more grateful to Him for the price that He paid to purchase us.

STEP SIX : THE SLAVE CONDEMNED TO DIE

Yes, the Lord of glory gave away everything to become a slave in order to purchase sinners for Himself. He had lost everything – all His rights as God, His freedom, etc. He had only one thing left – His life. He could have said, "Well, I have gone far enough. At least I should live." If He had said and done that, there would still have been something which He had which He had not used to pay for the treasure that He wanted. In remaining a living slave, He would have held His life back even though He had paid so much. By holding back His life, He would have lost everything, for there was one condition on which the treasure had to be obtained – the buyer had to give all that he was and all that he had. He had to give all, and then own all of the treasure. So even as a slave, Jesus accepted to die. He wrote a cheque with which to pay for the treasure, and part of that cheque was His life. He was, therefore, condemned to die as part of the payment, and He accepted it.

STEP SEVEN : THE WORST DEATH
DEATH ON THE CROSS

In writing off His life and accepting to die, the Lord Jesus was giving away everything. He had paid almost all that could be paid. However, one thing had to be settled. There are many manners of dying. He could die peacefully in His sleep. He could die honourably from some natural cause like sickness or an accident; then there would be no stigma on His name in death. But if He died honourably, He would hold back the last vestiges of His honour. He would have died honourably without shame. In dying that way, He could not have the treasure, because He had not abandoned all His honour in death. So if He was to have the treasure, He had to die the most shameful type of death, the type reserved for the foremost criminals. Then He would have nothing neither in life nor in death. The Lord looked at that treasure – you, the sinner - and wanted it so much for Himself that He accepted to die as the foremost criminal by death on the cross. By accepting to be hung on a tree, Jesus knew well that the Bible said, *"... a hanged man is accursed by God"* (Deuteronomy 21:23). He knew this and accepted it. He hung on the tree, cursed by man and cursed by God. It is beyond imagination what it must have meant to Him to accept to hang on the tree and be cursed by His Father. He could stand all others, but what about that one? To be cursed by God? Would He also pay it? Well, on it hung the treasure. He looked at you in your deliberate sin and He loved you and said, "I will accept to be cursed even by my Father that I may have this treasure."

As He paid all the price in life and in death, He became the possessor of all lost sinners. The power and authority over sinners passed from the devil back into His hands.

You were bought with a price.
You are precious beyond limit.
You cost Christ everything.
You owe Him everything.
Have you ever thought about that?

From the Cross to the Throne

The Lord Jesus, who wants to enter into a life-imparting relationship with you, is not only the Christ of the cross. He is also the Christ of the throne. He is no longer on the cross – dead. He is on the throne. There are also seven wonderful steps from the cross to the throne. The Bible says, *"Therefore God has highly exalted Him and bestowed on Him the name which is above every name, that at the name of Jesus every knee should bow, in heaven and on earth and under the earth, and every tongue confess that Jesus Christ is Lord, to the glory of God the Father"* (Philippians 2:9-11).

STEP ONE: THE RESURRECTION

God raised Christ from the dead. This was a far-reaching event. Death could not hold its foe. The temporary victory of death was soon overturned and the One who had died rose from the dead in tremendous victory. The Bible says, *"But in fact Christ has been raised from the dead, the first fruits of those who have fallen asleep. For as by a man came death, by a man has come also the resurrection of the dead. For as in Adam all die, so also in Christ shall all be made alive"* (1 Corinthians 15:20-22). The Lord is risen!

STEP TWO: THE RESURRECTION BODY OF CHRIST

Christ did not only resurrect and become what He was before He died. His resurrection body had far greater power than His body before He died. He could, in His resurrection, appear and disappear. He could pass through walls. He was no longer limited by the laws that limit matter. He was flesh and blood for sure, but He was flesh and blood plus something else. With that type of body which He did not possess before, He was another step up.

STEP THREE: THE ASCENSION

The Lord did not continue on earth with His wonderful resurrection body. He was not meant for earth. He ascended into heaven. The Bible says, *"As they were looking on, he was lifted up, and a cloud took him out of their sight. And while they were gazing into heaven as he went, behold, two men stood by them in white robes, and said, 'Men of Galilee, why do you stand looking into heaven? This Jesus, who was taken up from you into heaven, will come in the same way as you saw him go into heaven'"* (Acts 1:9-11). Jesus ascended. He is in heaven.

STEP FOUR: GOD HIGHLY EXALTED HIM

For thirty-four years heaven was as if empty. The Lord Jesus was away. There was a time when God the Father, God the Son and God the Holy Spirit could not hold their normal meetings. God the Son was away. There was a time when angels, archangels, cherubim and seraphim sought in vain for Him that they might worship Him. There was a time when the twenty-four elders yearned to fall before Him and cast their crowns before Him, but it was all was in vain. He was not there.

So can you imagine this absence for about thirty-four years? Can you imagine the longing of God the Father, God the Holy Spirit and all the heavenly beings for thirty-four years? Then one day He appeared! It was wonderful. What a union! What adoration! What worship!

Then I imagine that God the Father stepped forward and took God the Son and exalted Him. No, He did not just exalt Him;

He highly exalted Him. He exalted Him to heights of honour, glory, and adoration as were hitherto not attained. Yes, God highly exalted Him. It was not the exaltation of man. It was not the exaltation by man. God exalted Him. Hallelujah! Hallelujah! But was that all? Certainly not!

STEP FIVE: GOD GAVE HIM A NEW NAME

There is no doubt that the Lord Jesus had many glorious names in His right as God before He came to earth to die on the cross. When He got back to heaven, He immediately got back His names, honours and titles. But that was not all. The Father gave Him a name. It was a name that He did not have before. It was a name that no one had had before. It was the highest name in heaven. God Himself called it Lord and Jesus called it His new name; for Jesus in the Scriptures says, *"He who conquers, I will make him a pillar in the temple of my God; never shall he go out of it, and I will write on him the name of my God, and the name of the city of my God, the new Jerusalem which comes down from my God out of heaven, AND MY OWN NEW NAME"* (Revelation 3:12). Yes, the Lord Jesus had risen and been exalted to the highest glory of heaven. But that is not all.

STEP SIX: EVERY KNEE SHALL BOW

The name that Jesus received was of such might and authority that every knee must bow to it. The bowing is at three levels and it includes all created beings.

1. Every knee in heaven shall bow without exception. There

is no problem there since in heaven all are loyal to Him and bow to Him willingly.

2. Every knee on earth shall bow. This includes all human beings. Even those who do not believe in Him shall bow. Even those that do not want Him shall bow. All human rebels shall bow. You shall bow. There are some who do not want to bow now. They are too proud now to bow. However, a day is coming when all shall bow. Even from the lake of fire, all human beings who are lost shall bow. Why don't you bow now in repentance and be saved? Is that not the wisest thing to do? Why must you wait to bow from hell? Nevertheless, whether you bow now or not, you shall bow, for "At the name of Jesus every knee shall bow … of things on earth." Again we repeat: You shall bow.

But bowing shall not be done by heavenly and earthly creatures alone. Every knee of things under the earth shall bow. This concerns the kingdom of Satan. Every knee in that kingdom shall bow too. Principalities, powers, world rulers of this present darkness, mighty fallen angels, big and powerful demons, small demons and all kinds of evil spirits shall bow to Jesus.

Yes, He is Lord. The Bible says, *"Then comes the end, when he delivers the kingdom to God the Father after destroying every rule and every authority and power. For he must reign until he has put all his enemies under his feet. The last enemy to be destroyed is death. 'For God has put all things in subjection under his feet'"* (1 Corinthians 15:24-27). Even if these wicked spirits do not bow now, they shall bow from hell. The question is whether you will bow now and be saved or you will wait until then and bow with them from the lake of fire. That choice confronts you today.

STEP SEVEN : EVERY TONGUE SHALL CONFESS THAT JESUS CHRIST IS LORD

It is possible to bow without confessing with the lips. There is great power and there is also great humiliation in lip confession. Some would like to bow to Jesus and not open their lips to confess that He is Lord. Well, that will not be allowed. The angels in heaven and all other heavenly creatures shall confess very gladly and joyfully that Jesus Christ is Lord. The redeemed on earth shall equally confess with joy that Jesus Christ is Lord. The rebels on earth shall confess that Jesus Christ is Lord from the lake of fire, and the devil and all his host shall also confess that Jesus Christ is Lord. This shall be the greatest confession of all time and as God the Father shall see every knee bowing to Jesus and confessing that He is Lord, His joy and glory shall be fulfilled.

Yes, Jesus has been exalted, and the honour He has now is greater than the honour He had before coming to earth. The honour He will receive in all of eternity will far exceed that which He would have had had He refused to sacrifice everything in order to purchase the treasure of great price. He is indeed Lord.

CHAPTER II

The new humanity - 2 : A pearl of great value

The Lord Jesus told a second parable immediately after the one we have just considered and the two parables complement each other. He said, *"Again, the kingdom of heaven is like a merchant in search of fine pearls, who, on finding one pearl of great value, went and sold all that he had and bought it"* (Matthew 13:45-46).

We said that the treasure of great price was the sinner and Jesus gave away everything in order to purchase him. The Pearl of great value is the Lord Jesus and the sinner must also purchase Him at great cost by selling all that he has. It is quite obvious that the Lord Jesus has infinite value. He is the King of kings. He is the Lord of lords. All knees shall bow to Him. It is, therefore, life's greatest blessing to have a relationship with Him.

Many people wrongly think that they do not have to "pay" for Jesus. This is not correct. They have to "buy" Him at great cost. He has bought the sinner at the price of His all. The sinner must respond by "buying" Jesus with his all.

THE SINNER IS A MERCHANT

A merchant is rich. Each sinner is rich. He is rich negatively and he is rich positively. To purchase Jesus, the sinner must bring all his negative and all his positive wealth to the Lord Jesus.

He must bring all his sins without hiding any that he can remember. They may include the following:

1. Fornication.
2. Adultery.
3. Masturbation.
4. Immoral thoughts.
5. Immoral language.
6. Pornography.
7. Lying.
8. Exaggerations.
9. Anger.
10. Wrath.
11. Wickedness.
12. Abortions.
13. Homosexuality.
14. Lesbianism.
15. Petting.
16. Bitterness.
17. Strife.
18. Unforgiving attitude.
19. Selfishness.
20. a) Covetousness.
    b) Love of money.
21. Greed.

22. Jealousy.
23. Quarrelling.
24. Fighting.
25. Revengefulness.
26. Gossip.
27. Slander.
28. Mocking God.
29. Unbelief.
30. Mocking believers.
31. Persecuting believers.
32. Ignoring God.
33. Stealing.
34. Cheating.
35. Corruption.
36. Giving bribes.
37. Receiving bribes.
38. Pride.
39. Haughtiness.
40. a) Boastfulness.
    b) Pretence.
41. Cowardice.
42. Murder.
43. a) Favouritism.
    b) Injustice.
44. Nepotism.
45. Laziness.
46. Indiscipline.
47. Harshness.
48. Cruelty.
49. Faithlessness.
50. Instability.
51. Mercilessness.

52. Disobedience to God's Word.
53. Disobedience to God.
54. Disobedience to leaders.
55. Disobedience to parents.
56. Envy.
57. Idleness.
58. Gluttony.
59. a) Drunkenness.
    b) Foolishness.
60. Sorcery.
61. Witchcraft.
62. Magic.
63. Secret societies.
64. Idolatry.
65. Palmistry.
66. Grumbling.
67. Wicked thoughts.
68. Lovelessness.
69. Hatred.
70. Carelessness.
71. Stinginess.
72. Rudeness.
73. Vanity.
74. Egotism.
75. Self-righteousness.
76. Self-justification.
77. Self-advertisement.
78. Self-praise.
79. Spite.
80. Dishonesty,
81. etc.

The sinner must bring any of these that are found in his life. He must bring all the sins and sinful attitudes that are in his life to the Lord. He must not hide any of them. He must expose all of them to the Lord. The Bible says, *"He who conceals his transgressions will not prosper, but he who confesses and forsakes them will obtain mercy"* (Proverbs 28:13). If you have been living in an immoral relationship with a man or a woman, bring that one and yourself to the Lord and say to the Lord, "Lord, here I am and here is the partner of my immoral action. I surrender myself and I surrender my partner to You". (Your partner might not be present. However, do not neglect to surrender him/her all the same. Do it in prayer. God will then take over). You might have stolen money and bought a house, a car or some other thing. Say to the Lord, "I bring my sin of theft and I bring to You the stolen article or the article acquired with the stolen money. I leave all of it at Your feet." You might have cheated and obtained a false diploma. Bring the diploma to the Lord and say to Him, "Lord, here is the diploma, which is the fruit of my dishonesty." You must do this for everything in your life.

You must not only bring the things that you acquired wrongly. You must bring to the Lord those that you acquired rightly. They are included in all that you must bring along as part of the price to be paid for Jesus the Pearl of great value. You dare not keep anything away. Everything must be brought to Jesus. Everything, everything, everything. He will decide what is to happen to them, and He must have everything and decide about everything. If you keep anything back, you have disqualified yourself and you will not have Jesus the Pearl of great value. A rich young ruler once came to Jesus. He wanted to "purchase" Jesus. He wanted to have a relationship with Jesus. He wanted to have eternal life. Jesus demanded that he pay the full price for the Pearl of great value. He told him, *"One thing you still lack. Sell all that you have and distribute to the poor, and you will have a treasure in heaven; and come, follow me"* (Luke 18:22). It might have been easier for him if the Lord had said to him, "Go, sell a part of your goods and give to the poor…" The Lord did not say that, for if He had said that, He would have been deceiving the rich young ruler; for at that price, he would never have had Jesus. He had to give all to have all of Jesus. Jesus is not in bits so that people can give part of the price for part of Him. Either they have all of Him, or they have nothing, nothing at all. Either they pay the whole price, or they deceive themselves. The Lord Jesus told His disciples on another occasion, *"Fear not, little flock, for it is your Father's good pleasure to give you the kingdom. Sell your possessions, and give alms; provide yourselves with purses that do not grow old, with a treasure in the heavens that does not fail, where no thief approaches and no moth destroys. For where your treasure is, there will your heart be also"* (Luke 12:32-34). Who is not to fear? To whom does the Father have the good pleasure of giving the Kingdom? The answer is, "To the little flock." Who are the little flock? What are their characteristics? They are those who have sold their possessions and given alms. They have, in doing so, provided themselves with purses that do not grow old and will never grow old. They, by so doing, have provided themselves with a treasure in the heavens that does not fail and where no thief, moth, inflation, etc., can destroy it. Because their treasure is in heaven, their hearts are also in heaven, in the full and complete security of the Father. All others who have not obeyed this command are not the little flock. They must fear. They do not have the Lord Jesus.

So, if you belong to Jesus, you must "pay" with all that you have. Of course all people do not have the same things, but all must bring all that they have in order to "buy" Him. If all you have is ten francs, then bring it. That will do. If all you have is ten million, bring it. It will do. If you bring nine million out of ten million, it will not do. Do you have a bank account? Bring it to Jesus with all the money in it. He must become its Owner. If not, He does not own you. Do you have only five hundred francs, bring them. Do you have a house or several houses? You must bring them as part of the price. Do you have landed property? A plot? A farm? Bring them. Do you have a car? A fridge? A stove? A bed? Chairs? Boxes? Clothes? Bring them. What else do you have? Bring it. Bring it all of it.

Do you have a job? Bring it too. Do you have some certificates? Bring them too. They are part of the price to be paid. Do you have intelligence, practical skills, and abilities? Well, bring all of them. They are part of the price that must be "paid" in order to have Jesus, the Pearl of great value. Yes, you bring them and leave them at the feet of Jesus. Your right over them ends and you wait before Him for further instructions.

But is that all? No! You cannot yet have Jesus, the Pearl of great value. There are other things left. Do you have a wife or a husband? He or she must be brought and surrendered to Jesus. She/he is part of what you have and, therefore, part of what must be paid to have the Pearl of great value. Do you have a father, mother, mother-in-law, father-in-law, cousins, children, grandchildren, brothers, sisters, aunts, uncles, loved ones, friends, etc.? You must bring them to the Lord Jesus. You must bring all of them. You must not hold any back. They are all part of the price that you must pay to have Jesus, the Pearl of great value.

Is that all? Let's see. Do you have a family, a tribe, a country, a continent to which you belong? Well, these are all part of the price to be paid. Bring your family, tribe, country, continent, etc., and surrender them to the Lord Jesus. Do you belong to a club, society, organization, political party, etc.? These, too, are part of your possessions. They must be brought to Jesus and surrendered to Him. Without that the price would be incomplete and you can, therefore, not have the Pearl of great value.

Is that all? Do you have good looks, manners, wisdom, and any other attributes? Are you kind, gentle, loving, tender, caring, warm, disciplined, faithful, etc.? These are some of things that you must bring along. They are part of the price that must be paid in order to have the Pearl of great value. So bring all of them at once. Nothing can work without you bringing them.

Maybe you are saying to yourself, "Jesus is very costly." Well, indeed He is. Remember that He is the King of kings. Is it not normal that He should be costly? On the other hand, think of the price that He paid to purchase you. Did He not leave all the glory of heaven? Did He not go right to death on the cross? Did He hold anything back? Certainly not. He is not asking you to do anything to purchase Him that He did not do to purchase you. He is not asking you to bring anything that you do not have. He asks you only for what you have, but He demands all that you have. Is that not fair?

Now the deal is about to be settled. You have brought everything that you have and everything that you will have. But there is just one thing left. You must finally and presently bring yourself. Your very life, your self must be brought. Jesus said, *"So therefore, whoever of you does not renounce all that he has cannot be my disciple"* (Luke 14:33). He further said, *"If any man would come after me, let him deny himself and take up his cross and follow me.*

For whoever would save his life will lose it; and whoever loses his life for my sake and the gospel's will save it. For what does it profit a man, to gain the whole world and forfeit his life? For what can a man give in return for his life?" (Mark 8:34-37).

Will you bring everything that you have, that you are and your very self? Will you bring it now and surrender it to that Jesus who went to the cross to buy you for Himself?

Will you bring yourself and everything you have now? If you are willing, you can come to Him now, bringing everything and bringing yourself. Hand all over to Him. Give all to Him, including yourself You will then own nothing. You become His slave for Him to do what He wants with you. You also give Him your very life. So you bring to an end all that is of you as you give Him your all.

When you hand everything over to Him, you will have nothing and you will be nothing. He will immediately give you Himself, the Pearl of great value. With that Pearl Jesus, is included all that Jesus is and all that Jesus has. So you immediately pass from a state of poverty, having sins, sinful attitudes, earthly things and yourself to a glorious state, having none of these things but Jesus in His totality.

In this way, all of Jesus becomes yours. His nature becomes yours. His wisdom yours; His power yours; His riches yours; His glory yours; His resurrection yours; His enthronement yours; His exaltation yours; His past yours; His present yours; His future yours. You lost everything, yet you have received everything. That is wonderful. Yes, truly wonderful. His desires become your desires; His will becomes your will; His ambition becomes your ambition; His plans become your plans. Where He goes becomes where you go. What He says becomes what you say. What He does becomes what you do. You and He become totally united in time and in eternity. This is what becoming a Christian means. Will you become a Christian on these terms? If not, do not deceive yourself with any half measures. They will take you nowhere. They will bring you nothing that is truly of Christ and that is truly permanent. If you come on His terms, you will be blessed indeed. Will you come? Won't you come?

PART FOUR

CHOOSING YOUR PERFECT LIFE PARTNER

1. GOD HAS A PERFECT PARTNER FOR YOU
2. KNOW YOURSELF
3. SPIRITUAL COMPATIBILITY
4. PHYSICAL AND SEXUAL COMPATIBILITY
5. COMPATIBILITY IN HABITS.
6. INTELLECTUAL COMPATIBILITY
7. ARE YOU IN LOVE? ARE YOU LOVED ?
8. RECEIVING THE CONFIRMATION THAT YOU ARE THE PERFECT PARTNER FOR EACH OTHER.
9. COURTSHIP IN THE CENTRE OF GOD'S WILL

CHAPTER 12

God has a perfect partner for you

When a person makes Jesus Christ, the Pearl of great value his choice and comes to Him in absolute and unconditional surrender, he enters into the centre of God's perfect will for him. To continue in that perfect will, a person has to continue to seek the will of the Lord and obey it. Absolute surrender to Jesus as Lord at the very beginning of the Christian life is only the beginning of a process that must be lived day by day, hour by hour, and minute by minute.

To the surrendered person, we say that the first thing to do is to find out what God's perfect will for him/her is. It could be that His will for you is that you serve Him as a single person. If that is the case, He will give you the power to do it with joy and, therefore, you should give no further thought to marriage. What it means is that from the very foundation of the world, God saw that you could best serve Him and be fulfilled yourself by being single. He, therefore, did not create a helper fit for you. He is your helper fit. Can you then imagine the tragedy that would be yours if you got married to someone? The marriage would surely fail, not because you are a bad person or the partner is bad. It would fail because God did not ordain it. It was not His perfect will. It would never fully satisfy you. Even if you were fully satisfied, God's eternal purpose for you would be thwarted, and what a shame! Can you imagine the children who are born from such a marriage? They are children born outside God's perfect will. They were not meant to exist. If such children do not believe in the Lord Jesus and as a result go to hell, then by refusing to obey the Lord or by failing to discern His will, you have brought forth someone who will suffer forever and ever. Imagine the genealogy of such children – the genealogy of people who, in God's perfect will were never meant to exist. This is a most serious matter, and you should think about it seriously. Do not rush. Think. Even if you want to forget about the progeny from such a marriage, think of your own misery. You will wake up one day to find that you have made a mistake and you will have on your hands someone whom you will never be able to get rid of. Your union with that person would be like being tied to a corpse for life. You may inject formalin into the corpse. It will, however, always end up decaying. You may apply all kinds of perfumes, but the odour of the corpse will be there to follow you all your life. So we say emphatically that there is nothing whatsoever to be gained from a marriage that God never intended to take place.

If, on the other hand, the Lord shows you that His perfect will for you includes marriage, then you have the serious responsibility of finding out whom your perfect life partner is. It is obvious that God, taking into consideration everything about you, has made a partner for you who is His perfect life partner for you. Yes, the partner is there, made by the Lord and known by Him, and she is for you. Choosing a perfect life partner is searching for and discovering that person whom God has searched for, discovered and set aside for you. God has already gone through the difficult job of searching, discovering, and choosing the perfect life partner for you. His special one for you is available. She has been specially prepared for you, so that, like a rib taken out of you, she will fit perfectly at all levels – spiritually, intellectually, emotionally, sexually, etc. She has been so well chosen that she will satisfy your varying needs with passing years and changing circumstances. You do not have to ask God to make her. She has already been made so that in each other you will find perfect fulfilment.

Although she is there and known by the Lord, you do not know her. You have to search for her, find her and choose her. You may say, "Why does God not just make things easy for me by simply bringing her to me, so that I do not go through the difficult process of searching for her, finding her, and choosing her?" Well, the answer is that God is training you for rulership with Jesus. Part of the training is that He allows you to do things for yourself.

If He just dictates things to you, you will never be ripe for the throne. God also wants you as His co-worker, a co-worker who accepts and carries out responsibilities. So the process of choosing your perfect partner is part of God's training programme for you.

You may say, "That is alright, provided He ensures that I do not make a mistake." Well, He will not ensure that you do not make a mistake. He will not ensure that you choose rightly. You must make sure that you choose rightly by choosing what He has chosen. He is treating you as an adult. Must He not? One thing, however, is sure: If you are totally obedient and apply yourself well, you will find the one He has in store for you.

A. YOU MUST CHOOSE

Why does God not just bring the wife He has for you along and say, "Brother X, here is the perfect life partner that I have for you"? If He did that, you might one day complain about the fact that you were not allowed to choose. Adam complained when he said, *"The woman whom thou gavest to be with me, she gave me fruit of the tree, and I ate"* (Genesis 3:12). He declined all responsibility for the action she led him into because he was only the tool of the woman. So God will not impose His choice on you. In a sense, He considers you as sovereign, and this includes the freedom of choice.

In the Bible, Jacob wanted Rachel and was frustrated when they gave him Leah. He worked until he had Rachel, whom he loved. The Bible says, *"A prudent wife is from the Lord"* (Proverbs 19:14). But this prudent wife from the Lord has to be found. The Bible again says, *"He who finds a wife finds a good thing, and obtains favour from the Lord"* (Proverbs 18:22). *"A good wife who can find? She is far more precious than jewels"* (Proverbs 31:10). A good wife has to be found. She will be obtained as the result of diligent searching.

B. YOU WILL HAVE WHAT YOU HAVE CHOSEN

God is prepared to guide you in your search and in your choice. He promises to do so. In His word He says, *"I will instruct you and teach you the way you should go; I will counsel you with my eye upon you. Be not like a horse or a mule, without understanding, which must be curbed with bit and bridle, else it will not keep with you"* (Psalm 32:8-9). The Lord will instruct. He will guide. However, you must be obedient and you must have understanding. Again the Word of God says, *"Do not be foolish, but understand what the will of the Lord is"* (Ephesians 5:17). You can receive the Lord, be surrendered to Him, and yet be foolish and fail to understand His will. If you are like that, you will choose the wrong partner and suffer because of it.

Someone may say, "Well, I will just marry any believer. Anyone will be alright. We are the children of God." This is simple foolishness. It is like saying, "I have two shoes and two feet. I can just wear any shoe on any foot." Now, how comfortable will you be if your left foot is put into the right shoe? Will you have a bad time or not? The same thing can happen in marriage. A person who has received the Lord must not just marry anyone from the opposite sex who has received the Lord; for any member of the opposite sex is not your perfect life partner or your helper fit.

God expects you to co-operate with Him and, first of all, let your character be what He wants it to be. He also expects you to co-operate with Him in finding out whom He has for you as your perfect life partner. If you decide to be so foolish that you refuse to co-operate with God in finding the one whom He has in store for you, and you go about it foolishly and marry someone else instead of that special person who was made for you, you will reap the fruits of your folly.

I believe that the question on your heart now is, "Now that I know that God has called me into a married life, how can I find out who my perfect marriage partner is?"

Here are some suggestions on how to go about the whole affair:

- Know yourself.
- Find out which believer of the opposite sex is compatible with you in the following ways:
  - Spiritually,
  - Intellectually and maturity-wise,
  - Sexually and physically,
  - Habits, etc.
- Find out the most compatible one who also finds you compatible.
- Discover God's will about the matter.
- Be in love.

CHAPTER 13

Know Yourself

If you are going to be looking for a helper fit for yourself, then the first thing to think about is not what you want in the partner, but what you are and what you have to offer to the partner. Without this knowledge of yourself, how can you talk of a helper fit? How can you talk of compatibility? How can she be a helper fit for an unknown quality of yours? Can she be compatible with the unknown?

It is foolish to say, "Because God can do anything, I will just look for anyone and He will do the rest." It is also foolish to think that He will just look at your desires and then give you someone who will satisfy those desires. What of the desires of your partner? Will they be satisfied? Will you be able to satisfy them? Is God not also concerned about her desires and about their being satisfied? There is another matter that all must bear in mind. Although God can do everything, He will not just do anything. He will only do those things that are consistent with His nature and His will. Do not close your eyes and choose the wrong person, and expect God to perform a miracle that will make your relationship harmonious. He will not do that. Therefore, know yourself.

Know yourself spiritually. The following questions will help you :

1. Are you committed to the will of God without reservation? Can you offer spiritual leadership to a girl who loves the Lord with her whole being?
2. Have you made progress in the school of prayer? Will you be a prayer help to someone who is making rapid progress in the school of prayer, or are you still a baby? Are you divided at heart?
3. What is the one thing that God has called you to do for Him? What work will your wife help you to accomplish for Him?
4. Do you hate sin with your entire being? Have you been delivered from its dominion?
5. Do you give sacrificially to the Lord or are you still worldly, trying to go to heaven whereas you are infatuated with the world?
6. Do you obey the Lord step by step as His will is made known, or are you not yet decided on giving Him implicit obedience in all things?

Know yourself intellectually. Ask yourself the following questions; they will help you. What is my academic level through formal education and through informal education? To what type of person can I provide intellectual leadership? Whose intellectual ability would be an encouragement to me and not a threat? What ignorance would disturb me? What academic and intellectual level should my partner have that would best blend with what I have, so that God's call on my life will be best accomplished?

Know yourself emotionally. Ask yourself the following questions; they will help you. Am I an extrovert or an introvert? Am I withdrawn and is it difficult for me to open up, or am I often flowing freely? Do I make friends easily, or am I generally suspicious of people and slow to trust them? Do I easily recover when hurt, or do I brood over it for a long time? Do things, even small things, bother me, or am I not easily disturbed?

Know yourself sexually. Ask yourself the following questions; they will help you. Am I hot or cold sexually? Am I difficult to arouse sexually or am I easily aroused? What attracts me in a sustained way in the opposite sex? Am I attached to the members of the opposite sex that I come in contact with, or do I easily establish a relationship, break it, forget about it and establish another one?

Know yourself physically. Ask yourself the following questions; they may help you. Am I tall or short? Am I fat or slim? Do I have a capacity to become fat? If I have that capacity, can I be disciplined with food? What are my parents and grandparents like? What type of people of the opposite sex please me – the short, the tall, the slim, the light in complexion? Do I want a particular feature – long nose, beautiful teeth, narrow face, long legs, etc.?

Know your habits. Ask yourself the following questions and derive some help from your answers. Do I want things orderly and neat, or do I prefer them disorderly, or does it not matter to me? Do I prefer to be quiet, or do I like noise? Do I prefer to stay at home, or do I prefer to be on the move? Do I prefer to have visitors, or would I have people stay away? Am I extravagant, or am I thrifty? Am I quick and fast in speech, thought, action, or am I slow? Do I complain a lot or do I easily laugh at silly things and refuse to let them weigh me down? Do I easily adjust to new people, situations, places, ideas, or do I not want to have any changes? Etc.

Know your health condition. Ask yourself the following questions; they will help you to begin to think. Am I healthy or am I frequently sick? Do I have a serious handicap? What is it? Do I have body odour? How do I behave when I am sick? Do I take it easily or do I brood over it and get nasty to people and complain a lot, needing much attention? Do I sympathize with the sick, listen to them, comfort them and help them, or do I prefer to put the world between them and myself?

Know your ancestry. Ask yourself the following questions; they will help you out. Do I come from a broken home or from a healthy home? What was the relationship between my parents like? Were they loving, cordial, warm, and tender, or were they cold, hard and difficult? What are the main character traits of my family members and ancestors? Were they generous or stingy? Were they leaders or people of no consequence? Were they moral or immoral? Did they fear God, or did they treat Him lightly? How did they treat their wives and their husbands and children? Were they domineering or did they allow people to think and act freely? Were they orderly or disorderly? Were they dependable or not? Were they hard-working or lazy? Did they have many friends or were they often lonely, isolated people? What are my brothers and sisters like? What are their main characteristics? In what environment did I grow up - in a town or a village? In wealth or in poverty? Etc.

We could go on and on, but we shall stop here. After you have answered these questions honestly and clearly, you will have a clear idea about what you are and what you are likely to want in your partner. Because of the many variables that exist in God's creation, the perfect partner that God has for you will be able to satisfy you the most in all areas of your life, and find you satisfying in most areas of her life. In those areas where there is no immediate compatibility, both of you will have capacities to grow and adjust, so that even in those areas you will soon have harmony, for God is not a God of disharmony. He does not bring the disharmonious together.

Another thing to consider is that there are some things that are 'musts' for some people, while other things are 'mays' and that these things differ from person to person. Take as an example: Cleanliness is a must for some people, it is desirable for others, it does not matter for a third group of people, and there are people who will even prefer a dirty environment. So when God does bring people together in His perfect will, He will never bring people together who have extremely opposite characteristics, so that such people are prevented by their divergent characteristics from a harmonious relationship.

It is important to face these things and not to ignore them under the pretext that one is in love. People say that love is blind, but it is obvious that marriage is an eye-opener.

There are many things that people will be able to bear at the beginning, at the first flux of attraction, love, or infatuation with each other. However, this state of things does not continue indefinitely. You may say, "His voice caresses me." Let his voice caress you for now, but if he is careless with money, you may find it difficult to enjoy the caresses of his voice when he has carelessly spent all the money, and you, he, and the children are hungry and you cannot buy food.

You may be able to bear it now without complaining, but for how long will you bear? It is possible to carry a weight for one or two kilometres, but when that weight has to be carried for 100 kilometres or 1000 kilometres, that which was borne without any problem at the beginning may become a real burden.

ALL AREAS ARE IMPORTANT

Do not say that if the spiritual area is alright, you will serve the Lord and not bother about the other areas. All areas are interrelated. A dirty partner may cause you to be angry and not pray. A sick partner may stand in the way of your carrying out the one task that God has called you to do for Him, in addition to the fact that she may not put in the needed contribution. Therefore you should consider all these areas carefully because they will contribute to your success or failure in accomplishing that one call of God on your life.

CHAPTER 14

Spiritual compatibility

We strongly recommend that the spiritually incompatible should not choose each other. Their marriage will not work. If there is no compatibility in the spiritual realm that marriage can never satisfy the heart of God and, if the heart of God is not satisfied, all else will fail. People who are equally and totally committed will grow in increasing harmony as they press on towards the upward call of God. They will also grow increasingly distant from each other as they differ in their commitment to the Lord and to each other.

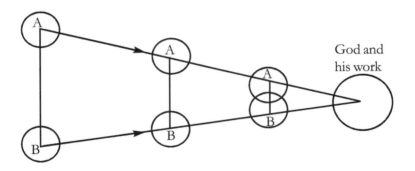

Fig. 10:

As A and B move increasingly towards the Lord and His work, they grow closer to each other, and their union is more complete. If one person stagnates while the other one moves increasingly towards the Lord, the gap between them will increase and their disharmony will increase as shown in Fig. 11.

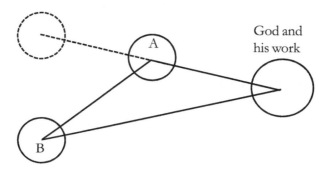

Fig. 11:
A gap is not only caused by one person stagnating. It is also caused by the union of two people who are at different spiritual levels.

Where there is spiritual incompatibility, you have something like the union of an eagle and a chicken. The eagle will want spiritual heights, having set his mind to *"seek the things that are above, where Christ is, seated at the right hand of God"* (Colossians 3:1). The chicken will set its heart on earthly things, be concerned with the present and passing. The result is that the chicken will pull the eagle down and the eagle will be a problem to the chicken. This incompatibility will affect all the other areas.

The chicken will want their money invested in earthly things while the eagle wants it invested in heavenly things, and there will be discord. The same discord will come in when they consider the investment of
their time,
their talents,
their energies,
everything indeed.
Finally, it will be a big conflict. The smaller the degree of in-

compatibility, the smaller the disharmony; and the greater the difference of spiritual commitment and vision, the greater the discord.

I say from personal experience and from experience obtained through counselling over a period of twenty years, that spiritually incompatible people should not choose each other. Their marriage will
fail. If one person wants to win a continent for Christ and the other one thinks that a village is already too much, how can they help each other?

Before you ask someone to become your partner, you should assess what your commitment is and what the person's commitment is. You should find out what you have of spiritual weight, spiritual history, knowledge of God, knowledge of His Word, passion for the lost, etc., to give to the person you want to marry. You should ask yourself if the person will be able to receive these things, for you should not throw pearls to the swine. You should also ask whether what you have will satisfy the person. You may have many things to offer but because of the person's maturity, what you offer will be like a child's play.

After you have analysed what you have to offer and how it will be received, you should carefully find out what the person has to offer and find out whether or not you will be able to receive it. It may be too much for you, or it may be too little.

A. THINGS MAY NOT CHANGE

Do not marry the person with the hope that the person will change in the future. There is no guarantee that he will change.

You must judge him by what he is today. If there is a big gap between you and him spiritually, how do you ever hope that it will be bridged? Even if he grows rapidly, do you not see that the gap will remain if you, too, continue to grow rapidly yourself?

All marriages that are based on the expectations that the person will change and become something else, will certainly fail. Spiritual growth is the function of spiritual vision. There is no guarantee that someone who does not see now will necessarily see more in the future. So be wise.

If you are committed to the upward call of God and to serving Him so that His heart is satisfied, do not lower your standard in order to be married. The Lord surely has a helper fit for you, and that one will most certainly be compatible with you spiritually. Wait. Do not rush. God is never in a hurry. If you have not yet found him or her, time is not up. You will be happier in the future for having waited.

It is better to remain single and serve the Lord alone than to be married to a chicken. I counsel you to look carefully before you choose. There are some big and fat chickens that make a lot of noise, and they may be mistaken for eagles. If you are an eagle, discern well because a chicken, even a fat and strong chicken, is not an eagle. When it comes to the very refined matters of following the Lord in the narrow way at any cost, the chicken will show forth the fact that it is a chicken and not an eagle.

If your purpose in marriage is to satisfy the heart of God, then you cannot take this matter of spiritual compatibility lightly.

B. WHAT ABOUT THOSE WHO ARE CHICKENS?

God has no place in His kingdom for those who will not go all the way with Him. He has no place for those who love this world and the things of this world, for they do not have the love of the Father in them.

God has no place for those who have refused the upward call of God. He has no place for those who will not commit their all to Him to serve Him. We said in the chapter entitled: "The New Humanity: A Pearl of Great Value" that those who do not bring everything and all of themselves to Christ, cannot have Him. Those half-hearted people, who are in love with the present world and would not pay the total cost in order to follow the Lord, are not really His children. They may be in the church. They may say this or that, but the Lord knows those who are His, and those who are His have forsaken all that they might follow Him.

If you are a chicken, which means that your surrender is partial and that you are holding back part of the price, you can do what you want. God will never be involved in your marriage. You are His enemy. You are His traitor. You, by your half-heartedness, are the devil's agent in the church. You are planted there by Satan so that you may destroy God's Kingdom from within. The Lord knows that you are Satan's agent. You are like Ananias and Sapphira, and you will soon face His judgement if you do not repent. Is today not the day for you to repent, bring your all and be accepted by Him? Must you let another day pass by, while with your divided heart you woo God's judgement on you? If you do not repent quickly, and that judgement comes upon you, do not say you were not warned. I am warning you today!

CHAPTER 15

Physical and sexual compatibility

Many people think that as long as there is spiritual compatibility, all other areas are not important. That is not correct thinking. Some think that sexual compatibility is of little consequence. In my opinion, it is the second most important area. To ignore it would be to court a disaster. Failure in the sexual life will cause trouble in many other areas. The unfulfilled wife will complain about other things, and the unfulfilled husband will find very many things unsatisfying. He will certainly stress on small faults which he would have otherwise ignored were he not sexually unfulfilled. Because physical looks have a close relationship with the sexual life, we have decided to treat them together. We shall start with the sexual aspect.

We know that some people are hot, others are warm, and others are cold sexually. If a hot woman marries a cold man, the woman will not be satisfied, and the man will feel inadequate because of his failure to satisfy her. The same thing happens if the man is hot and the woman is cold. It is clear that different people respond differently to different touches. Some want light touches, others want heavy touches. Some want sexual intercourse several times in one night. Others want it once a week, and we have had a case in our clinic of someone who wanted sexual intercourse once in three months. Some are totally carried away by the sexual relationship, giving themselves away totally, enjoying it to the fullest; whereas for others it can be an ordeal to be borne. Some people reach the orgasm very quickly, while others hardly reach any climax.

For those who are lost in sin, experimentation with many people may lead to a knowledge of some of the sexual capacities of possible partners. But those who are children of the light, those who have received the Lord Jesus in their lives, cannot carry out such acts of foolishness. How then will they know if they are sexually compatible? The answer lies in a close walk with God. Tell Him you cannot do anything in this area. Ask Him to give you the woman that you will be able to satisfy completely, and who will in turn satisfy you completely. You should then go ahead and look carefully into the other areas that you can do something about, and God will take care of the future.

Do not judge on the basis of what your experience was in the world before you came to the Lord. That experience is of the past and must be forgotten. The Lord has made you a virgin. You may find that your sexual capacities after conversion differ radically from what they were in the world. God has made you a new creation in every way.

What about physical compatibility? In the Bible we are told that Sarah was beautiful. She was so beautiful that even in old age she was desirable. We are also told that Rebekah *"was very fair to look upon"* (Genesis 24:16). Of Leah and Rachel, the Bible says, *"Leah's eyes were weak, but Rachel was beautiful and lovely. Jacob loved Rachel ..."* (Genesis 29:17-18). We strongly recommend that no man should ask a woman he does not consider beautiful to become his wife, and no woman should accept a man that she does not consider handsome. It is said, "Beauty lies in the eyes of the beholder." If that is the case, and it may be the case, regardless of what other people think of her, you should find her very beautiful and attractive. You must not marry someone you find ugly. You must not marry someone whom you will need to put the lights out in order to draw near to, because you do not like his or her physical appearance.

Physical looks play a greater role in life than most people want to admit, and believers must face it. Generally speaking, people prefer the company of someone they consider nice to look at. They also are more tolerant of the errors of such a person than of the errors of the person whose appearance annoys them. You must face that fact. If you do not like his looks, say, "No," to him. You must be firm. If you say that you will manage, some day you will be sorry about it. If you do not like her looks, do not marry her because of her good character. Some day, you will come face to face with her ugliness and, more so, you will see it in your children and be very sorry. If you do not like short people, do not say, "Yes," to a short person. Say, "No." There is someone who may consider him totally handsome, and you must leave him alone.

You should not just look at the present looks. If you do not like fat people, find out what the girl will look like after she has given birth to two children. Do not consider her slim when it is just due to the fact that she is overworked at school. Look at her older sisters and her mother, and it will give you some idea of what she will look like in the future.

If a man refuses to face these facts and marries a girl although he has reservations about her looks, a distance will build between them with time. He will find her less and less attractive. He will spend less and less time with her and draw close to her only out of duty. He will often find the sexual relationship with her boring. He will tend to kiss her less and less and, with time, their relationship will become cold and formal; and if they labour and grow in Christian character, the relationship will become one of a "brother and sister" and not one of a husband and wife.

If that were all, it would not be too bad. It could become worse. He may become attracted to others whom he considers beautiful, and may even fall into immorality in his thoughts an perhaps in actual deed.

It is not enough that your partner be beautiful in your eyes. You must find out whether or not your physical looks are pleasing to the person you are interested in. Ask her to describe the physical appearance of the person she has always thought should be her husband. See if you resemble that person. If you do not resemble the person in any real way, do not press her to accept you. She may say, "Yes," to you and become your wife, but all her life she will be looking for and yearning after that person whose appearance pleases her.

When a person wants someone with a particular physical appearance, he must bear in mind that this is a serious matter. He may adjust to some others or in the flash of the moment of infatuation forget what he wants, but he will come back to his senses and will desire what he originally wanted. Jacob preferred Rachel from the beginning. Leah bore him many children, while Rachel was barren. But the fact is that he only tolerated Leah all his life. He loved Rachel even when she was barren. He also loved Rachel's children, Joseph and Benjamin, in a special way.

Therefore, look carefully at yourself. Know what you want. Find out if you have the looks that the other party wants. If you satisfy her/his requirements and she/he satisfies yours, then you can go ahead.

One last word about this, one man told me that he married a slim girl and now he is forced to live with a fat woman who is three times the size of the girl he loved. How could he be expected to love her? This is important. Love, sex appeal, etc., are very closely tied up with physical appearance. You have the responsibility to labour and maintain that which made you pleasing to her or him in the beginning. If you were slim and now you are fat and massive, do you blame him for being cold towards you? If you were tall and slim, and now you are huge and have a big stomach from undisciplined eating, do you blame her for being unresponsive to your advances?

So you will have to labour to keep what you had, and much can be done in this direction. It is not only a matter of pleasing a partner. It is also a matter of pleasing the Lord and accomplishing your life's work. You have the duty to do all that you can to present to God the best physical form possible, for God loves beauty. In your grooming of yourself, of your clothes, your hair, everything, you must offer Him the best. A man who is careless with this physical looks, or a woman who is careless with her looks is reflecting a deeper problem. Looks talk of something deeper than looks. Do you read the message of looks? You should read it, for it is a warning. In marriage you will confront in the person's character that which careless looks warned you of. Do not say that I did not warn you.

I must add one last word. It is possible to be ugly and to hide it with clothes. I do not blame a person who does that. However, in marriage, you will not be facing the well-dressed person who was specially prepared for the meeting. You will meet the person as he or she is indeed. Try and see beyond the clothes and weigh what you think of the person. Look at yourself in the mirror, naked, and face what you have to give someone. Will it satisfy her? Will it satisfy him? Will the person without clothes be a shock to him or her? Is he or she mistaking your beautiful clothes for a beautiful or handsome person, or is there more to it?

When you have carefully looked into these matters, you will know whom to give yourself to and whom to receive. In God's eternal purpose, He has a partner whose looks will please you, and who will be pleased and satisfied with your looks, as you labour to cooperate with God in making your physical appearance the best possible.

CHAPTER 16

Compatibility in habits

Some people are organized, disciplined and orderly. Others are the exact opposite. These characteristics reflect something much deeper and, so, must be taken very seriously. If one partner puts things in an orderly way and hates disorder, and the other is disorderly, they will have serious problems. My advice is that such people should not choose each other. I have talked to orderly people who are married to disorderly people, and they each say that this is a real sore in their marriage. The orderly partner wants clothes to be well-hung and probably facing the same direction. The disorderly partner will throw them anywhere and promise to put them properly later on. The same thing will happen to the shoes, tooth paste that is not closed, rubbing oil that is open and the lid has disappeared, pants soaked in the basin for the brushing of teeth, pots opened and scattered; the fridge disorganized, water left partly running, the bed unmade or made in such a way that things are not symmetrical, books torn and scattered, money lying carelessly around, etc. Added to this disorder may be a bad habit that causes the clothes, house, and dishes to be dirty at all times. If you entered in the kitchen you might think that pigs had just had a celebration there.

Someone who is organized and disciplined and tidy will be frustrated with a disorganized, undisciplined and untidy partner. The matter becomes even more serious because the indiscipline and disorder will show itself in the bathroom, bedroom, kitchen, sitting room, car, and everywhere. A disorderly person has a capacity to put disorder into everything that he or she touches. It seems to happen so naturally. The organized person will try to put order into things while the other person more or less, unconsciously disorganizes them. This will lead to conflict. The parties in such a marriage will be unhappy. The disorganized party will live under the strain of the order that is being imposed on him from the outside, while the organized person will be frustrated by the disorder around. Disorderly people rarely change. They may try for some time, but it will not last. A disorganized person may spend hours putting his room in order, but no sooner is the task complete than he/she starts to scatter what was organized.

If in addition to being disorganized the person is also dirty, then the problem is made worse. We strongly recommend that no organized and clean person should marry a disorganized and dirty person. It will be the ruin of both lives, and possibly that of the children born into it. One partner may be able to bear with the other, but for how long? He may finally sink into being disorderly and dirty, but that will make him hate his partner and hate himself.

So before you choose a partner, ask yourself, "Am I organized or disorganized? Am I clean or dirty? Do I like order or disorder? Do I feel comfortable with disorder, or does it infuriate me? How do I react to dirt? Do I hate it completely, do I hate it partially, or does it not bother me?" When you have found out what you are and what you like, you know what you will be taking into the life of your partner. Will it bless her or frustrate her? Then look at your possible partner carefully. It does not take long to detect the signs of disorder. He may be well dressed, but you will notice carelessness somewhere. Look at his books. Are they scattered or organized? Visit his room. Look at his bed. Look at his shoes. Are they in pairs or are they scattered? Are they facing one direction or several? You will soon know what the person is like. You will then be in a position to make up your mind. Decide on whether you will bring blessings to the person in this area of his life or problems. Also decide whether the person, in being himself, will bless you or not. Do not say, "The person is disorderly. I will change him." You will not. If he is at home in disorder, you will make him unhappy by trying to change him. By introducing order you may ruin his manner of life. Do not say, "Let me marry that orderly person so that he can help me to be orderly." Do you know that you may ruin him? He may become quite frustrated in the process. So the best thing is to marry someone who is like you. But, better still, cry out to God so that your disorder, which really talks of disintegration at a deeper level, be healed.

Another important habit is the attitude towards people. Some people love the company of many people while others do not. If someone who loves happy company marries the morose and withdrawn type of person, he/she will have problems. I know of a brother who likes visitors and would like to invite people home for dinner. His wife wants only her husband and children around. They are incompatible in this realm. There was tension which finally blew up some day, and I had to receive them in our Clinic for Spiritual Diseases. Their problem was incompatibility.

Another area of possible problems is the union between a stingy brother and a generous sister. He calculates everything to the last franc and will even count sticks of matches if possible.

He does not want to give anything away. He wants to balance the family budget accurately to the third decimal. They say that he went to the University of "Economics, Stinginess, and Strict Accountability." The sister, on the other hand, is generous. She gives and gives and does not even remember to whom she gave the last lot of things. She can only give an account of ten thousand francs notes. When a ten thousand francs note is changed, she can no longer tell what happened to the thousands. Such a brother must not marry this sister. They are incompatible. He should look for a sister with similar characteristics, and the generous sister should wait for her perfect life partner from the Lord. He will have the same generous attitude, and not crush her with demands for accounts right to the last franc. He will trust her judgement and believe that although she does not remember in detail how the money was spent, it was wisely and honourably spent. It is not God's purpose to unite dissimilar people to their own detriment. Someone said that if you bring stones with sharp edges together and shake them together for a while, the sharp edges will go away and they will fit together. This may be true, but sometimes the stones break and scatter. To avoid such a risk and the unnecessary pain caused, people should look for compatible partners. Have you examined your attitude towards things? Do you know her attitude towards things? Will you fit together and glorify God? Think carefully before you act.

Another area of possible discord is that of food. There are some sisters who take food seriously. Even if they are alone, they take time to cook food well even if it is just a small quantity of food. They set the table well and get everything in order before they eat. There are others who will eat bread or anything that can be eaten in a hurry. They can hardly settle to cook properly, and when they do cook, it is poorly done. Now, consider a brother who wants food well-cooked and properly served. He will have a good time with the first sister as a wife, but will have constant problems with the second sister. It is not that anything is wrong with the sister or brother; they are just different. So, in order to avoid unnecessary problems, those brothers who are particular about food — how it is cooked and served — should know whom they ask to be their wives. There is also the matter of quantity. Some sisters count the grains of rice that they serve. In fact, a brother once confessed that his wife used to serve him such small portions of food that often he went from his lunch at home to a restaurant where he bought food and ate it in order to fill his empty and complaining stomach. Such differences should be looked into so that people know what they are getting into. This will prevent scandal in the house of God.

Another area of possible conflict is the way husbands and wives relate to each other. The husband may come from a family where love flowed. Each time the father of the home came back home, all would go out to welcome him — mother, children — and he would embrace each one in turn. The wife always treated the husband with deep respect and never ever pronounced his name. He in turn told the wife where he was going and when he would be back. He never left the house without giving details about where he would be even if he was going out for an hour. If such a man marries a woman who comes from the same type of background, then they will have a good time. However, if she comes from a background where no one went out to receive the father on his return home, where the mother did not as much as say, "Welcome," to Papa, but went about her affairs when he came back home as if nothing had happened at all, and often called him by his surname, then there will be conflicts. They may appear to be trivial matters, but one day he will blow up. To avoid such problems, look carefully into what you are getting into. Think very carefully about what you are, and about what you have to offer in this domain, and weigh things.

The family background often has a very big impact. The woman will treat you the way she saw her mother treat her father. You should check this in advance if you can. You will treat your wife the way you saw your father treat your mother. Therefore, you should find out how she will take it when you treat her that way. The family background of your wife or husband has had a telling influence on her/him. He grew up in that background for 25 years. She also grew up in her own background for about 25 years. So for better or for worse, he has grown in that kind of environment for that length of time. These people have influenced her character for all this time. It will be most difficult for her to change. It is not easy to straighten a tree that has been bent for 25 years. If you meet his relatives, take note of their attitude to things. Some of those attitudes and tendencies are surely in him even if they do not yet come to the surface. They will come. I know of a sister who always shocked me by her rude treatment of men. Then one day she told me of the way her mother used to treat her father. She was perfectly rude to him. Even though she was angry that her mother had treated her father so badly, she just did the same unconsciously. Of course, she will put on Christian character and eventually be different. If you want to suffer these shocks for all the years that it will take her to change, then marry her. If you do not want such problems, look for someone else whose background is similar to yours. I am quite surprised that with increasing time I see myself unconsciously doing things the way my beloved father did them. The proverb says, "Like father, like son." There is some truth in it.

In the past, parents used to study families before they allowed members of their family to be married to members of those families. This was rooted in the sound theory that children will behave like their parents. The modern generation has thrown this away to their own undoing.

You should be careful. Do not marry someone who is incompatible with you and then start praying that God should change that person. He has not made such a promise to you. He has not told you to marry just anyone you want and He will change the person to suit you. What about Him changing you to suit the person? Who should be changed? You or her/him?

Intellectual compatibility

One brother who could hardly spell his name (he did not have the primary school leaving certificate) went to a young lady in the assembly who had done post-graduate studies to near the doctoral level and told her that he wanted her to be his wife, since both of them loved the Lord. He said that he had dreamt about it and so felt that the Lord had prepared that sister to be his perfect life partner. It turned out that his appearance was repulsive to the lady in question, and so the other areas were not thought about, for the brother was told at once to forget about it.

As I thought about the incident, I remembered another young man I had met. He was a graduate in the Liberal Arts. He was a very intellectual type of person. He spoke and wrote French and English fluently. He had a high capacity to appreciate poetry. When he read the Bible, he was absorbed, not only by the spiritual content, but also by the language of the Word. His wife did not complete secondary school. She was not interested in reading. She was just a warm, loving, beautiful village girl. Needless to say that the marriage was not going smoothly. He was very lonely. He could not share many things with her. She would not understand. Her stories were about who had had a baby, whose wife had done what; these things were of no interest to him. She, too, was lonely. They were otherwise very nice people, but they were intellectually incompatible.

Before a man should think of choosing a particular girl, he should ask himself the following questions:

1. What is my intellectual level? What certificates do I have?
2. How much formal education do I have?
3. With what intellectual group of people can I fit in and communicate without feeling inferior?
4. Am I inclined to intellectual matters?
5. Do I enjoy the realm of ideas or the realm of things and people?

These questions will help you to discover yourself. There are some people whose level of formal education is low, but through informal education they have brought themselves up to a very high standard and can, thereby, fit into any kind of company. There are others whose intellectual education has really stopped at the level of their formal education. There are people who may have big certificates, but they are fundamentally villagers at mind. They are not intellectual at all, even if they hold a doctorate's degree. There are others who, though unschooled, are very philosophical in their approach to every discussion.

You should analyse yourself well and truly know yourself. You should then be in a position to say which type of woman would fit a man like you. She should be able to satisfy you intellectually, depending on what you are intellectually. So do not just look at the certificate. Look at the total education of the person and see where it fits with yours. Ask yourself whether you will be able to satisfy her intellectually. If you will not satisfy her intellectually, or if she will not satisfy you intellectually, then you are not her perfect life partner; for how can the perfect life partner fail to satisfy in such an important area of life? If she is very simple-minded, she may not be able to understand God's call on your life. How can she help you to accomplish that which she does not understand? If your vision and call are global and she has no capacity to see in that dimension, how can God be the author of your relationship? If she thinks of conquering the world for Christ through literature, and all you see is a small village assembly of 20 people, how can you be God's choice for each other? What will she help you to accomplish?

If she is sophisticated, she will need to be wooed in a sophisticated way. You will need to be able to tell her in a hundred different ways that you love her. You will need to woo her with words, flowers, poems, etc. How will you satisfy her if these things are totally above you? If he needs a poetic breakfast and a romantic supper, how can you provide these if you do not know what they are? If you are so different in depth of mind, do you see that you will not have much to talk about?

What are your cultural similarities and dissimilarities? I was visiting a town when two lovers who were having problems came to see me. The boy complained that the girl did not love him. The girl said that she loved him very much, but he would not understand. I asked the girl to tell me how she manifested her love to him. She told me, "I write him a love letter every day. I have composed many poems that talk of my love for him. I sing him songs of love. I buy him small presents and I go to see him often." I then turned to the boy and asked him what he wanted. He told me, "She has never cooked certain types of food in her house and brought them to me. She does not come to wash my clothes and iron them. When there is a misunderstanding between us and it is proved that she is wrong, she writes a long letter of apology with a song inside, but this does not mean much to me. I expect her to prepare me an 'egusi' dish as a token of her repentance."

As I listened to them, I knew that even though they might be in love, they were cultures apart. The problems they were having would multiply in marriage and affect many other areas in their marriage. Although both were university graduates, one was an untouched villager and the other was a modern girl. Their union would fail. He would be unsatisfied with her expression of love, and she may never be able to do what he wants her to. He did not tell me what he did to express his love for her, but I can imagine that it would be crude and leave her unsatisfied. Her feelings are obviously refined and his are crude. Will it work?

Something else that I would like to mention here is the matter of maturity. Some people mature intellectually and in their total person very early, whereas others never mature at all. You can have a mature man of 21, and another one that is still a child at 40. This same thing applies to women. Before you choose a life partner, do not just think of your physical age. What is your maturity age? Are you 5, 10, 15, or 25 years old maturity-wise? Once you settle this about yourself, then think about the other person. What is her actual maturity? She may be 20 years of age and have the maturity of a 25-year-old, whereas you may be 30 years of age but have the maturity of a 5-year-old. You may say, "Well, I am 10 years older than her, so I will make her my wife," but do you realize that although you are 10 years older in physical age, you are 20 years younger in maturity age? How do you think a man like you, with the maturity age of a 5-year-old can offer leadership to a girl who has the maturity of a 25-year-old? Do you not see that it will just not work? It could be the opposite, that she is 28 years old but is still 4 years old in maturity age. She sulks, withdraws into herself, changes with the weather, and is not dependable. If you are 30 years old in physical age and 25 years in maturity age, do you not see that this 28-year-old baby of 4 years maturity age is not the perfect partner for your life? Do you not see that that is not the person that God has for you, even though she may be shouting and complaining about her old age? Do you think that you can parade your 4-year-old baby into the work of God and expect her to be the one who will offer you all the help you need to be and accomplish all that God called you to do for Him? Not to think about this area as well is to make a serious mistake. It is even more serious when you consider the fact that it will be close to impossible to redeem the situation. Take the first man, for example. His physical age is 30 and his maturity age is 5. For every six physical years, he grows one maturity year. In order to be able to do those things that a man should do at 21, he will need to be 21 x 6 = 126 years. You, therefore, have to wait a long time! Do you want to waste your life waiting for a big baby to grow up? Think carefully. I have warned you. You are incompatible. Save yourselves from trouble and save the Church from trouble by ensuring that you do not choose each other. Let the big baby marry another big baby. They will have less problems together. As for you, marry an adult and do adult business for God.

There are other areas like compatibility in health, attitude to children, discipline, etc., but I will leave you to use the principles of self knowledge, what the other party can offer, and what you have to offer to work out these areas too.

You will not forget to consider what your sexual history has been. If you have gone to bed with a host of men or women, that is part of your history, which must not just be thrown away. If you have had children with other people, this must be considered. You will also find out what the sexual history of your possible mate has been. Has she gone out with many men? Was she treated of venereal diseases? Did she commit an abortion? Has she any children? With whom did she have the children?

You may say that the Lord has forgiven these sins that were committed while you were lost in sin, and that on that account they should not be mentioned. I agree with you that the Lord has surely forgiven them and that His forgiveness is thorough. However, you should face the fact that marriage is not just a spiritual issue. Even though the Lord has forgiven, there may still be the practical consequences of the sin. If a young man was rendered sterile by a venereal disease and He is forgiven his sin, his sterility is not automatically taken away. He needs to be healed of this. If he had five children with five different women, the woman that he now wants to marry must know this and decide whether or not she loves the man enough to start life with him, with 5 children aged between 4 and 12 from 5 different women. So the sexual history should be investigated and known. Marriage is not an altar of sacrifice, and each person must know what he has to give away and what he has to receive, and weigh things prayerfully before God.

FINDING THE MOST COMPATIBLE PERSON WHO ALSO FINDS YOU COMPATIBLE

At this point you should know yourself very thoroughly – what you are, what God has called you to do, the certainty that He has called you into the married life, what you have to give, and what different members of the opposite sex have to give.

It is obvious that it will take a long time to do this, and that you must do it prayerfully and use all your God-given intelligence. Because the person you marry will affect your life so profoundly, you owe it to God and to humanity to carry out this holy exercise seriously. It will take time. It will take some action. It will take asking questions; it will take analysis; it will take finding out facts, but all of that is important.

After all, people spend a lot of time studying different models and finding out things like gas-consumption, availability of spare parts, after sales service, etc., before they buy a car which they can get rid of any time they want. Is it not folly to do less when it concerns the person you will be bound to for all of your life, and who will be the one single most influential factor in your life, next only to the Lord Jesus? Fools will not find out. They rush where angels fear to tread. You are not a fool. Find out. Your happiness may depend on how effectively you found things out. Consider the spiritual life, for example. How will you know if she is a chicken or an eagle? You may see a fat chicken at meetings and mistake it for an eagle, but a more thorough analysis to know the depth of her commitment to suffer for the Lord, give sacrificially, hate sin, separate herself from the world, know the Word of God, and all the other things, could show the fact that her heart is set on heavenly things. If you do not find out, you will not know.

You will arrive at one person whom you will satisfy the most and who will satisfy you the most. This will be based on your long study and research.

However, you have not yet reached the end of your search. You have to find out if you love the person and if the person loves you.

CHAPTER 17

Are you in love ?
Are you loved ?

Many people speak of falling in love. They talk of it as a "fall." That is why they often fall out of it. That is also why, because it is a fall, a downward motion, they do many foolish things when they are fallen. My advice to you is that you should not allow yourself to fall in love.

People say that they saw somebody for the first time and their heart suddenly went out of control, and all their being began to yearn for the person in such a way that they could not control themselves. They could not eat, sleep, think, etc. All they wanted was that person. Some people fail examinations at the University and at school because they say this thing they call "falling in love" has happened to them. Others throw themselves away hopelessly at the feet of these people they say they have "fallen" in love with and allow anything to happen to them. They no longer find out what the person is, where he is going to in life, what he is committed to, what he can offer, etc. It is as if the person had thrown a spell on them and they were no longer the same. Now this is a most dangerous thing. No child of the God dares allow himself to so "fall" in love. First of all, the person concerned may be an unbeliever. Secondly, because the one is swept off his feet entirely, he may not be able to ask God what He thinks about it. He may just ruin everything. People who "fall" in love in such a manner are sick. They need to be treated. Many such experiences are the fevers of people whose hearts and emotions are uncontrolled. It is a manifestation of gross indiscipline. One thing that often happens is that after some time the fever wears off and the person recovers and is healed. Once healed, he may not find any real worth in the person for whom he thought himself dying for. The same person is likely to "fall in love" with another person in the same way and, therefore, go from one such experience to another. I just want to say that such people are most dangerous. Anyone who cannot keep his head, who cannot control his emotions, who cannot direct or redirect his feelings, is hopelessly immature. The thing is this: such a person can be married to you, and one day when you are out together, he sees another person and suddenly that spell called "falling in love" comes upon him, and he either leaves you to throw himself at the feet of the person, or he comes with you, but his heart and all are no longer with you. They are gone with the person. Some people say, "You have stolen my heart." Hang the thief!

In my travels, I once met a young woman who was very beautiful, clean, educated, and accomplished. She was just a very lovely person in every way. She is among the most near-perfect people I know of, and she is a child of the King of kings, saved by the blood of Jesus. I asked her if she was praying that God should give her a life partner and she said, "No." I further asked her if the Lord had called her to serve him in the single state and again she said, "No." Later on she told me that she once loved a man who refused to marry her and married some other girl. She said that she had loved only that man and would never love another man. She would, therefore, live her life that way. I asked her if she had tried to love another man. She replied that she had hardened her heart against the possibility of loving any other man. That first man whom she loved and who did not love her must remain her only love. As I thought about it I saw this as another type of that folly people call "falling in love." She loved somebody. The person preferred someone else, and is possibly very happy with the person he has married. Instead of saying to herself, "Well, I thank God that I loved him and I love him. I wish both of them happiness together. I will always love him but I will open my heart so that my love can flow to another person," she has assigned herself to a useless emotional martyrdom. This is folly. Because I talked to her very many times, I know she can love again. There is no one who is so constructed that he can only love once. In fact, a person can love many people. It will not be all to the same degree, but it is there. It need not be the same degree either.

A. LOVE MUST BE A HEALTHY CONTROLLABLE EMOTION

Many people speak of falling in love. They talk of it as a "fall." That is why they often fall out of it. That is also why, because it is a fall, a downward motion, they do many foolish things when they are fallen. My advice to you is that you should not allow yourself to fall in love.

People say that they saw somebody for the first time and their heart suddenly went out of control, and all their being began to yearn for the person in such a way that they could not control themselves. They could not eat, sleep, think, etc. All they wanted was that person. Some people fail examinations at the University and at school because they say this thing they call "falling in love" has happened to them. Others throw themselves away hopelessly at the feet of these people they say they have "fallen" in love with and allow anything to happen to them. They no longer find out what the person is, where he is going to in life, what he is committed to, what he can offer, etc. It is as if the person had thrown a spell on them and they were no longer the same. Now this is a most dangerous thing. No child of the God dares allow himself to so "fall" in love. First of all, the person concerned may be an unbeliever. Secondly, because the one is swept off his feet entirely, he may not be able to ask God what He thinks about it. He may just ruin everything. People who "fall" in love in such a manner are sick. They need to be treated. Many such experiences are the fevers of people whose hearts and emotions are uncontrolled. It is a manifestation of gross indiscipline. One thing that often happens is that after some time the fever wears off and the person recovers and is healed. Once healed, he may not find any real worth in the person for whom he thought himself dying for. The same person is likely to "fall in love" with another person in the same way and, therefore, go from one such experience to another. I just want to say that such people are most dangerous. Anyone who cannot keep his head, who cannot control his emotions, who cannot direct or redirect his feelings, is hopelessly immature. The thing is this: such a person can be married to you, and one day when you are out together, he sees another person and suddenly that spell called "falling in love" comes upon him, and he either leaves you to throw himself at the feet of the person, or he comes with you, but his heart and all are no longer with you. They are gone with the person. Some people say, "You have stolen my heart." Hang the thief!

In my travels, I once met a young woman who was very beautiful, clean, educated, and accomplished. She was just a very lovely person in every way. She is among the most near-perfect people I know of, and she is a child of the King of kings, saved by the blood of Jesus. I asked her if she was praying that God should give her a life partner and she said, "No." I further asked her if the Lord had called her to serve him in the single state and again she said, "No." Later on she told me that she once loved a man who refused to marry her and married some other girl. She said that she had loved only that man and would never love another man. She would, therefore, live her life that way. I asked her if she had tried to love another man. She replied that she had hardened her heart against the possibility of loving any other man. That first man whom she loved and who did not love her must remain her only love. As I thought about it I saw this as another type of that folly people call "falling in love." She loved somebody. The person preferred someone else, and is possibly very happy with the person he has married. Instead of saying to herself, "Well, I thank God that I loved him and I love him. I wish both of them happiness together. I will always love him but I will open my heart so that my love can flow to another person," she has assigned herself to a useless emotional martyrdom. This is folly. Because I talked to her very many times, I know she can love again. There is no one who is so constructed that he can only love once. In fact, a person can love many people. It will not be all to the same degree, but it is there. It need not be the same degree either.

B. LOVE CAN DIE

Love is like a plant. If it is given the right nourishment, it will grow and blossom. If given the wrong food, it will die. It can also die from starvation. It is not true to say that if you love a person indeed, you will always love the person. If the love is not nourished (and it is best nourished when it is responded to and the person flows back in return), it will die. Some people mistake love that has been killed for false love. This is not so.

It is because love must be nourished or else it will die that we insist that the relationship be harmonious. Many conflicts will shock love and kill it. The shock of discovering the person for what he is instead of what you thought he/she was, may kill the love. Harshness, neglect, thoughtlessness, lack of contact, etc., will help to kill the love. Broken fellowship with God will certainly cause love that had Him as its Source to die. One hymn writer says, "By many deeds of shame, we learn that love grows cold." This is the lot of many marriages. They were begun in love. One or both parties were careless. He/she possibly took the other party for granted. He/she did not watch his/her looks, words, purpose in life, etc. and, gradually, the flow stopped and the tender plant died.

C. LOVE CAN BE KEPT GROWING
FOR COUNTLESS YEARS

We have seen that love can die. But love need not die. Love can grow from one degree of glory to another with passing time. However, for this to happen, both parties must commit themselves to keep it aflame. They must rekindle it. They must pour new oil into it to keep it blazing. The following things will cause love to keep growing and to blaze more and more:

1. An increasing commitment to remove the things in your life that the other person does not like.

2. An increasing commitment to build the things in you that the other party likes.

3. An increasing capacity to recognize your faults, own up to them, ask for forgiveness instead of justifying them.

4. An increasing willingness to be the loser in an argument or disagreement.

5. A commitment to take the first initiative towards reconciliation, regardless of who is wrong.

6. An elimination of criticisms that are not constructive and about which nothing can be done.

7. An increasing commitment to love the Lord, get rid of all sin and serve Him in total humility.

8. An increasing capacity to praise what is praiseworthy in the other person and to cover his/her faults about which nothing can be done. If, for example, the person has some defect that cannot be changed, you should never talk about it.

9. An increasing exchange of tokens of love – small gifts, letters, poems, visits, glances, etc.

10. An increasing confession of love not only by deed, but also by word.

D. Are you in Love ? Are you Loved ?

You are now in a position to tell whether or not the person who is compatible with you so far loves you, and if you love the person in return. This is a crucial test of compatibility. You may be compatible in everything else, but if you do not love each other, then there is no future for your relationship. You should not just marry someone because he/she and you have a lot of things in common. It will not work. Love is like the oil that keeps the engine of the car going. Without oil, even the best engines cannot function. Without love, even the most compatible people will not hold together in a marriage relationship. If the person does not love you, do not press the person into saying, "Yes." What is the use of a "Yes" that is forced out of the person? Normally, if the relationship has been well-handled up to this point, then both parties will be anxious to confess their love for each other. However, before they take this final step, I recommend that they do two more things.

E. Expose yourselves to each other

Until now you have been finding out things about each other indirectly or directly with discretion. There will be things about each other that the other party does not know, which they ought to know. They may be so important that they could make him/her change his/her mind. He must know. He must not be tricked into marrying you. He must come into the marriage with full knowledge. It is also better that you get the facts from each other rather than gather them from the distorted fragments of tale-bearers.

Find a time to be alone. Have enough time to be together. Pray to the Lord to help you to speak the truth, to speak all the truth, and to hold nothing back or play over facts.

The boy should speak first and then the girl. What things should be included in this self-exposure? I recommend the following :

1. Your previous sexual experience.
-    Are you a virgin ? Who made you lose your virginity?
-    How many men/women have you been involved with? Who were they ? What was the extent of the involvement?
-    Any pregnancies that led to a miscarriage or a criminal abortion?
-    Any children born?
-    Any venereal diseases? The extent of the treatment and cure.
-    All fears in the realm of sex.
2. Your general health condition.
-    Your general state of health.
-    All the diseases you have had and the extent to which they were treated.
-    Any and all the diseases which members of your family have had.
-    Any symptoms of diseases that you have.
-    All your fears in the general area of sickness.
3. Your financial situation.
-    Your total wealth - be very specific.
-    Your debts.
-    All your assets.

- All your liabilities and to whom you are liable.
- All your vows to God.
- All your special commitments to your family and to others.

4. Your previous involvement with
- sorcerers,
- magicians,
- palmists,
- anything that has to do with the occult.

5. Your friends and your enemies.

6. The deepest spiritual ambitions in your life.

- Those things that you consider as 'musts' in your life, which you must do for the Lord.
- Any special things that God has called you to do for Him.
- Your most private spiritual experiences.

7. All the other things that are in your life which are important.

If after this you still want to go on, then there is one last step before you are fully committed to each other.

CHAPTER 18

Receiving the confirmation that you are the perfect partner for each other

The last thing is God's will about the matter. It would seem that if you get to this stage in your relationship, then you are probably meant by the Lord for each other. There are three things that should be used as confirmatory signs, and I consider them important.

They are:

1. The peace of God.
2. The opinion of the leaders of the local assembly that walk in the power of the Lord.
3. The opinion of the parents of both partners.

A. THE PEACE OF GOD

The Bible says, *"And let the peace of Christ rule in your hearts, to which indeed you were called in the one body"* (Colossians 3:15). As you pray about your relationship, if it is of the Lord, His peace will reign in your hearts. You will be perfectly at peace that the Lord is leading you together to become husband and wife, and that you are therefore in His perfect will. If, as you pray and walk before Him, you have doubts or your spirits are disquieted, then it is a sign from the Lord that something is going wrong. Stop and find out. For the peace of the Lord to serve as a sure confirmatory evidence, you must both be walking in purity before Him. If you sin deliberately and will not confess or forsake that sin, then the Lord will leave you to yourselves. You may have some peace, but it is not the confirmatory peace of God. Rather it is the silence of God who has said, "Because you will not walk before Me and be perfect, I take My leave and leave you to yourself." It is of primary importance that you be totally honest with God and with each other. If one of you is having the slightest feeling of uncertainty, that one must speak out. Both of you may not have the same degree of spiritual sensitivity. The one who is more sensitive may receive warning signals first. Let that one not hide them. Let him speak.

It is useless to carry out a marriage that is not in the centre of God's will. If you do so, you will suffer on earth and suffer in the life after death. Every minute of your life will remind you of your folly, and you will be sorry for it. You may later on meet the person that God had in store for you, and with whom you would have had a perfect marriage union; but you will not be able to marry that one because you gambled away your opportunity on the altar of disobedience and haste. So, if you are going to be fully certain of the Lord's will, both of you must be unreservedly surrendered to the Lord about it. You must say to the Lord and to each other, "We shall continue this relationship only as long as we can, with the fullest conviction, say that it is the will of God. We shall call it off any moment we know that it is not His will, regardless of what it may cost us or cost anybody else. We have no other desire but to do the will of God, regardless of what that will may be."

When people say this to the Lord and to each other and mean every word of it, the Lord will guide them and keep them in the centre of His will. If He allows their relationship to continue, it will be because they are His perfect choice for each other.

B. THE OPINION OF THE LEADERS OF THE LOCAL ASSEMBLY

In a local assembly where believers walk close to God in sensitivity to the anointing that they have received, and whose elders are men after God's heart, their opinion will often be very indicative of the will of God. I can say that we have evidence over the last four years that in every relationship about which the elders expressed concern and asked the people to stop or to wait, and the parties continued or insisted on having their way, these people found out shortly after marriage that the elders were right, and wished they had obeyed. Anyway, they have a long time to wish they had obeyed. It is very unlikely that a team of prayerful elders who walk with God and serve Him in the integrity of their hearts, will be wrong in their opinion about a couple they know well. Sometimes because some prefer to ignore them, they just keep quiet about some relationships. This does not mean that they approve of the relationship. They have just decided to act like God in the situation and let people have what they lust for and reap the resulting consequences. What else can they do? They are not to fight with people. They are to guide those who seek to be guided. My advice to you is that you consider the advice of your elders as the voice of God speaking to both of you about the matter. You may say that you are burning. I advise you to put out the flame and listen to counsel. If you don't, one day you will find that the flame is no longer there, and that which was fire then is an ice pool now in which you are being submerged, and that for how long ?

C. THE OPINION OF YOUR PARENTS

I see things more clearly now and understand God's ways of guidance more clearly now than I did some years ago. I also understand the principles of spiritual authority more. I strongly recommend that you consider the opinion of your parents as indicative of God's will for you. It does not matter whether or not they are believers, but the matter takes on new proportions of importance when they are believers. So, regardless of what your parents may be – pagans or Christians, educated or illiterate, civilized or primitive – I suggest that you consider their opinion as indicative of what God has in store for you.

I am not saying that the reasoning of your parents will always be correct. It often will not be. Actually, their reasoning does not need to be correct to be an indication of what God has in store for you. They may, for example, oppose the relationship that you want to establish. They may say, "We do not want this boy or this girl. He/she is not from our tribe." Or, they may give some other stupid reason. I advise you to take their opposition as indicative of the voice of the Lord that says that the person you have chosen is not the right one.

The problem is not the fact that he/she is not from your tribe, but the opposition of your parents is a suggestion that God does not want the relationship. Their reasons are wrong, but the facts should be taken seriously.

I am now more convinced that when people have gone ahead in spite of the opposition of their parents, they have later on come to wish they had listened. I know numerous examples of marriages where the parents had opposed the relationship for one reason or the other. Because the reasons sounded stupid and the parties were quite taken up by each other, they brushed aside the parental opposition and got married. Later on in the marriage relationship, they came across difficulties and situations that, although totally unrelated to what the parents had said in the beginning, were enough problems which, had they foreseen them, they would have stopped the relationship at once. I remember a young man whose marriage was a failure, saying, "I wish I had listened to my beloved father. He gave me other reasons for not wanting the relationship, but I thought I was wiser. Now I know that I was wrong and that in his ignorance he was yet being used to help me out of what I now know to be a wrong relationship."

It is interesting to know that when God is in the centre of a relationship, He causes parents who normally would have opposed the relationship for tribal or other reasons to give their warm and wholehearted approval to it from the beginning. The hearts of the parents are in the hands of the Lord, and He turns them in any direction that He wants. When the parties miss hearing His voice directly, He moves the leaders of the local church to refuse their approval or He moves the hearts of the parents to oppose it. Sometimes He moves both leaders of the local church and the parents to say, "No," to the relationship. The sad thing is that some people have still pressed on to have the relationship to their undoing.

I advise you to take the opinion of your parents seriously. You will one day know that you would be happier had you listened to them. A word to the wise is sufficient.

When the peace of God reigns in both your hearts and the

counsel of elders of the local assembly give their approval, and your parents are at peace with your proposals, I feel sure that you can make a total commitment to each other without reservation - the Lord made you for each other. You are each other's perfect marriage partner. You have found each other. Go ahead in obedience to the Lord and you will be blessed.

CHAPTER 19

Courtship in the centre of God's will

There is a time that elapses between that moment when the two parties have made a total commitment to each other to become helpers fit for each other, and the day when they appear before the legal authorities and the people of God and are declared husband and wife. I call that time the time of courtship.

That time is of such far-reaching importance that it must be handled well, so that the future may be a continued blessing. The fact that things have been well-handled so far should encourage the parties to press on in the fear of the Lord, fully assured that He has the best in store for them.

A. LENGTH OF COURTSHIP

I suggest from hard-earned experience both from my own life and from very many cases which I have had to counsel in different parts of the world and especially in the Clinic for Spiritual Diseases, that the courtship should be short. A few months are enough. There are many reasons for this.

The first reason for this is that there is temptation to fall into the sins of :

1. impure thoughts,

2. impure touches,
3. impure embraces,
4. impure kisses, and the worst could happen,
5. fornication.

Because the believer must be pure in thought, word and deed, any impure thoughts and actions are tragic. They ruin the relationship with God and with each other (I shall come back to this point later on). The commitment to each other raises the desire to have the relationship consummated in sexual union. To make the commitment and then wait for years is tempting each other. No one is too strong to fall at least into the sin of impure thoughts, and this ruins the relationship with the Lord of holiness who demands holiness from within.

The second reason why the period of courtship must be brief is that the two people may grow apart. At the moment of mutual commitment to each other they may indeed be compatible, but over the many months and years, they may so grow in very different directions that they become unsuitable for each other, but they are held together by their commitment to each other which honour compels them to keep, even when the relationship has ceased to be a joy.

Take, for example, a young man and a young woman of the same degree of spiritual maturity and commitment to the Lord. They are engaged, but they do not marry. They boy leaves the country and goes to another country where the spiritual climate is different. His spiritual growth rate is greatly reduced. The girl continues to grow steadily in the Lord. Her relationship with the Lord grows deeper and deeper, and she is increasingly delivered from all sin and the love of the world. After three years, they meet again. They are engaged. They have to get married. There is no spiritual compatibility anymore. It is a kind of marriage between the eagle and the chicken. She knows that it will not work, but she had given her word, and as a person of honour she feels that having given her word, she must suffer the consequences by keeping her promise. This is not a blessing.

Take another example. The parties part. At the time of parting as fiancé and fiancée, the boy had 'A' levels and the girl had 'O' levels. The boy goes abroad. After seven years he comes back with a doctorate's degree. The girl has not made much progress. She has been a nursing aid in a small hospital. They meet after seven years. They are almost strangers to each other. They are intellectually incompatible. Their social experience is very different. They are incompatible. The boy has met another girl abroad. He loves her deeply. They are totally compatible, but he cannot marry her because he must keep his promise and marry the girl he left back home. They get married, but they will not be fulfilled. There are barriers to spiritual fellowship and social union.

The third reason why I strongly discourage long courtships is that they are time-consuming. The Christian is at war. He is fighting against Satan and his army. He is called upon to redeem the time. Courtship is very costly time-wise and, also to some extent, it is financially costly. Let us take the matter of time first. The time that lovers spend together very often cannot really be justified in the light of all that needs to be done in the Kingdom of God. Even when the parties are disciplined, there will always be time that is spent together which any honest evaluation must describe as wasted. When the parties are separated, there is the time that is wasted in writing so many letters, time that could bet-

ter have been put into the work of the Kingdom of God. Sometimes there are misunderstandings that take time to make up,
and because the lovers feel a fresh touch of love when quarrels
have been made up, they tend to be more in love and, therefore,
waste more time together. For people who do not see the rea-
lity of the battle into which a Christian is born and grows, what
I am saying will sound like nonsense, but those who see it know
that I am talking about an important issue. So, when you calcu-
late the time put into each other in a week, which may be three
visits each lasting two hours, and multiply it by fifty-two weeks,
you will find out that 312 hours have been wasted. If this goes
on for five years, then that becomes 1,560 hours. Can you imagine the waste? Can you imagine what great things could have
been done for God with that time? Apart from the time that is
spent together, is the time that is spent alone dreaming of each
other, or talking to people about each other. You cannot have
abandoned, surrendered your all to purchase Christ, the Pearl of
great value, and then waste His time in this way without realizing
that you are sinning.

The fourth reason why long courtships must be discouraged
is the financial costs involved. Can you imagine the money that
is invested by lovers on the art of courting? Can you imagine the
money that one person spends on air tickets flying from one
continent to the other just to see the beloved? Can you think of
all the taxi fares? Can you work out the cost of all the gifts? Can
you work out the cost of all the things that a lover has to buy
for himself or for herself in order to be especially pleasing to the
one he loves? Can these expenditures by a disciple be justified
in the light of the great commission of the Lord and the world's
millions who are without the gospel witness, partly because of
limited finances?

The fifth reason for which long courtships are not advised is the emotional waste. Courtship is often carried out at a high emotional gear. This emotional energy that is invested on a girl or boy for years could have been better invested on the Lord Jesus and the work of winning the lost.

The last reason why I discourage long courtships is that they limit social development. When a person is engaged, his capacity to interact with people of the opposite sex is necessarily limited. There is a lot that can be learned from wholesome and free interaction with members of the opposite sex. If you are engaged at 20 to be married at 27, you have 7 years in a cage and some of what you would have learnt is lost permanently.

One final thought: What if the whole thing fails after all these years of focusing on one person who never becomes your partner?

In view of these reasons, I strongly recommend that all people who are not thinking of getting married in the near future should refuse to be committed to anybody in particular. They should enjoy the company of the opposite sex in a general way, guard their hearts and invest their all into loving the Lord and doing the work of the Kingdom. They will surely be greatly rewarded for this when the Lord comes, and even in this life, when they get married, they will be more richly blessed.

B. Purity in Courtship

It is important that courtship be conducted in all purity. The Lord of glory is looking for purity in the heart. Dirty thoughts are an abomination to Him. He said, *"Every one who looks at a woman lustfully has already committed adultery with her in his heart"* (Matthew 5:28). We can also write, "Everyone who looks at his fiancée lustfully has already committed fornication with her in his heart." Or, "Anyone who touches her fiancé lustfully has already committed fornication with him in her heart."

Is the best way to prepare for marriage to fornicate? Would you have God's fullest approval by so acting? Is that the best way to prepare for the future?

Normally, kissing, long embraces and touching some parts of the body will lead to impure thoughts. Do not think that you are believers and so your bodies will respond differently. You are still flesh and blood, even though you are indwelt by the Holy Spirit. You have no vaccine against impure thoughts if you encourage them.

I strongly recommend that all lovers talk it out and write down the following rules about their courtship. They should read them out to each other each time they meet and should obey them.

1. We shall not kiss each other before we are married.
2. We shall not embrace each other when we are alone.
3. We shall not touch those parts of our bodies that may arouse sexual desires.
4. We shall refrain from going to places where we shall be tempted to begin to tamper with each other's bodies.
5. Each time we meet, God's angels surround us. We must, therefore, never do anything that would cause them to withdraw with heavy hearts.

6.   We must wait until we are married before we begin to explore each other.
7.   We shall lose nothing by waiting. Rather we have everything to gain.
8.   We shall not violate these rules even if other Christians are behaving in a contrary way and justifying their sin.

There is another thing about this whole matter of purity (I discussed it more fully in Book One of this series entitled: "Enjoying The Sexual Life"). I shall just say a word or two here. Even when no fornication in action is committed by two lovers, their unholy caresses, embraces and kisses do harm to their relationship. When a girl allows a boy to touch her neck, breasts, and so on, they may both be apparently enjoying it but, in the boy's heart, the girl sinks in value. He is disappointed that the girl he is going to marry is so cheap and so accessible. He may even wonder whether she has not been allowing other men to touch her in the same way. He may continue with her, but she has far less value before him than if she had not allowed herself to be touched. He expects less from her and his general expectation of fulfilment in the marriage is lowered.

God's law has the force of a natural law and more. He demands purity because He is pure. He also demands purity because the impure destroy themselves. You should obey God's law, or else you will break yourselves on it.

You may say that this is very difficult, but the best is reserved for those who receive strength from Christ to do that which they could not do on their own.

C. WHAT LOVERS SHOULD DO DURING COURTSHIP

I suggest that the lovers should make very clearly defined plans in the following directions :

1. Improving the quality of their relationship with God.
2. Building each other up where there is need for improvement.
3. Labouring to be a blessing to society.

1. IMPROVING THEIR RELATIONSHIP WITH GOD

Each partner should say, "I want to enable my partner to be the person after God's own heart as much as possible." I suggest that they work out a scheme of reading the Bible together. They will assign themselves a certain number of chapters to read everyday and, when they meet, they should share what they got out of it. They should not cover up any laziness, whether it is that of one person or of both of them. They should work out a scheme for Bible memorization and carry it out. They should greet each other with a Bible verse instead of a kiss. They should plan long fasts together. They should arrange to meet regularly and pray. They should work out an evangelistic schedule and carry it out together and have many spiritual babes together. If they have talents that can be used to serve the Lord and the work of the gospel, they should use them together, like singing duets, etc. They should decide together if they want to stand behind the ministry of some apostle, prophet, evangelist, pastor or teacher. When they choose the person, both should stand together behind the person with their prayers, gifts and encouragement. Everything should be done to prevent spiritual growth in different directions and spiritual ministry in different directions.

2. BUILDING AND STRENGTHENING EACH OTHER WHERE THERE IS WEAKNESS

Shortly after you have committed yourselves to each other, I encourage you to make a list of each other's greatest weaknesses and show each other and agree on them. There is no use pretending by saying, "Everything in you is so perfect that I see no weakness whatsoever." That is the language of a fool. His eyes will soon be opened. It is also a mark of dishonesty or fear to call things by their names. If you do not do this, you will not help your partner. When each has accepted the weaknesses, you should both ask for the willingness to change (strangely enough, there are many people who love their weaknesses and would not want to part with them. There are others who neither love them nor hate them, while there are others who hate them, but will not pay the price needed to get rid of them). Pray together. Each one should tell his/her weaknesses to the other while the other party helps him/her by supporting him/her in prayer.

The next thing is that you should work out what you are going to do to get rid of each weakness. The plan that is worked out will depend on what type of weakness it is. There should be regular check up. Encouragement should play a significant role. Do not run each other down, but be firm where the other is running away from needed discipline. Be patient. Some of the weaknesses have been there for years. It will not be easy to get rid of them in a short time. Rome was not built in one day. The important thing to look for is progress in the right direction.

I suggest that you should also make a list of each other's strong points and work on making them stronger. There are no limits to the possibilities open to growth.

Seek God's help in all these, especially in separate and joint praying. It would help to find a spiritually mature person who loves both of you and is prepared to commit himself to be your counsellor and friend. It is recommended that you both agree on the person and stick to that person. Throwing your problems to every person shows immaturity and indiscipline.

3. LABOUR TO BE A BLESSING TO SOCIETY

You are in the world. It is God's world. Do not withdraw from it. Be involved. After all, marriage is only for here and now. There will be no marriage when the Lord Jesus comes. I suggest that you select some area of ministry that will help you to build each other up. I suggest something like visiting the sick together, praying for them, witnessing to them, supplying their needs either directly (from yourselves) or indirectly (by exposing their needs to others and getting them to give you the things that these need for you to take to them). Show them the love of God.

You can, on the other hand, prefer to minister to handicapped adults or children. Or, it could be that your burden is for prisoners. Ask the Lord to show you where you should invest your love for the world. It will pay dividends. Some will come the Lord, and all will receive some practical help. When you have chosen the area of ministry in which you want to be involved, stick to it. Do not move from one thing to the other. Do not just seek excitement. It would hurt them if you went only once or twice, or if you went to them irregularly. Your presence, your words, the love of the Lord which you take to them will mean much to them, and who can receive these and not begin to look forward to the next visit? Do not think that it will be easy. There will be setbacks. You will meet some that are ungrateful, but you are not seeking your own pleasure. You are ministering life, and the ministry of life is very costly.

Finally, visit people and places. Learn. Enjoy God's world – parks, zoos, lakes, etc. Keep God in the centre. He has given you everything to enjoy.

Stay in Love.

Work out plans for the wedding.

Be married.

Remain in love !

If I stand before Christ's judgement seat

1.   If I stand before Christ's judgement seat
And the Lord should open the Book of Life
If He should look in vain for my name
And not find it there where it should be

If my name were found on many diplomas
And my picture on many front pages
If I had been honoured by many rulers
Of what use would that honour then be?

2.   If all the wealth of the world were mine
If I had more money than all the rich
If I were surrounded with all luxury
And knew only times of ease on earth

What would all that wealth serve at the moment
When before the Judge I stand condemned
What would that luxury and ease have served me
When naked and poor I'm cast into hell?

3.   If I were surrounded with many worshippers
The young and beautiful yearning for my love
If I should be surrounded by many friends
And be the centre of all attraction

What would all those many worshippers serve
When alone I face the dreadful Judge
Who of all of them would stay with me at that time
When in hell I am all loneliness?

4.   Now is the hour of God's salvation call
      The voice of the blessed Saviour calls me now
      I will go to Him no matter at what cost
      And receive His love and pardon just now

      Then all my sin will be gone forever
      And the blessings of heaven will be mine
      Then to live on earth totally for Him
      And to love Him who first loved me.

Nkolbisson, March 9th 1984

Very important

If you have not yet received Jesus as your Lord and Saviour, I encourage you to receive Him. Here are some steps to help you,

ADMIT that you are a sinner by nature and by practice and that on your own you are without hope. Tell God you have personally sinned against Him in your thoughts, words and deeds. Confess your sins to Him, one after another in a sincere prayer. Do not leave out any sins that you can remember. Truly turn from your sinful ways and abandon them. If you stole, steal no more. If you have been committing adultery or fornication, stop it. God will not forgive you if you have no desire to stop sinning in all areas of your life, but if you are sincere, He will give you the power to stop sinning.

BELIEVE that Jesus Christ, who is God's Son, is the only Way, the only Truth and the only Life. Jesus said, *"I am the way, the truth and the life; no one comes to the Father, but by me"* (John 14:6). The Bible says, *"For there is one God, and there is one mediator between God and men, the man Christ Jesus, who gave himself as a ransom for all"* (1 Timothy 2:5-6). *"And there is salvation in no one else (apart from Jesus), for there is no other name under heaven given among men by which we must be saved"* (Acts 4:12). *"But to all who received him, who believed in his name, he gave power to become children of God..."* (John 1:12). BUT,

CONSIDER the cost of following Him. Jesus said that all who follow Him must deny themselves, and this includes selfish financial, social and other interests. He also wants His followers to take up their crosses and follow Him. Are you prepared to abandon your own interests daily for those of Christ? Are you prepared to be ledin a new direction by Him? Are you prepared to suffer for Him and die for Him if need be? Jesus will have nothing to do with half-hearted people. His demands are total. He will only receive and forgive those who are prepared to follow Him AT ANY COST.

Think about it and count the cost. If you are prepared to follow Him, come what may, then there is something to do:

INVITE Jesus to come into your heart and life. He says, "*Behold I stand at the door and knock. If anyone hears my voice and opens the door (to his heart and life), I will come in to him and eat with him, and he with me*" (Revelation 3:20). Why don't you pray a prayer like the following one or one of your own construction as the Holy Spirit leads ?

> "Lord Jesus, I am a wretched, lost sinner who has sinned in thought, word and deed. Forgive all my sins and cleanse me. Receive me, Saviour and transform me into a child of God. Come into my heart now and give me eternal life right now. I will follow you at all costs, trusting the Holy Spirit to give me all the power I need."

When you pray this prayer sincerely, Jesus answers at once and justifies you before God and makes you His child.

Please write to me and I will pray for you and help you as you go on with Jesus Christ

***

If you have received the Lord Jesus-Christ after reading this book, please write to us at the following addresse :

For Europe :

Editions du Livre Chrétien
4, Rue du Révérend Père Cloarec
92400 Courbevoie
Courriel : editionlivrechretien@gmail.com

Cet ouvrage a été imprimé
en janvier 2014 par

FIRMIN-DIDOT

27650 Mesnil-sur-l'Estrée
N° d'impression : 121283
Dépôt légal : février 2014

Imprimé en France